Everyone has their tra
love. Part of the motiv
this passionate, tumultuous journey details almost two decades of *Sex and the City*-esque dating adventures, disasters, and lessons. Equal parts funny and sad, these stories are filled with the relatable slices of hope, heartbreak, outrage, confusion, and self-discovery that most of us (no? just me?) experience in our search for love. You'll *definitely* laugh, you *might* cry, and I'm *almost certain* you'll learn a thing or two. All accounts are based on true stories. Names have been changed to protect the privacy of all those involved. And, of course, there are two (and sometimes three or four) sides to every story—this is just mine.

By: Sonia Acosta
Edited by: Rebekah Young
Cover Illustrated by: Laura Molina

© 2019, Sonia Acosta Self-Publishing

ALL RIGHTS RESERVED. This book contains material protected under International and Federal Copyright Laws and Treaties. Any unauthorized reprint or use of this material is prohibited. No part of this book may be reproduced or transmitted in any form or by any means, electronic or mechanical, including photocopying, recording, or by any information storage and retrieval system without express written permission from the author/publisher.

AUTHOR BIO: Sonia Acosta is a professional marketer and brand storyteller, eternal optimist, and life enthusiast who recently took her talents and sass back to her hometown in Miami after stints in Chicago and New York City. A proud Cuban American, Florida Gator, and

Loyola Rambler, she's been intimately involved in a lifelong affair with words. Full of feeling, passion, and an unstoppable resolve to live her best life and help others do the same, she craves to inspire readers through the raw emotion, candid detail, and sometimes scandalous humor of her real-life stories, struggles, and triumphs—even if that means being more vulnerable than most people can handle.

soniaacosta.com
#MyFunnySadLife

TABLE OF CONTENTS

DEDICATION..1

PREFACE..2

CHAPTER 1: Heartbreak: The Early Years...............6

CHAPTER 2: Two Boys, One First Love..................15

CHAPTER 3: Looking for Love in *All* the Places: The College Years...46

CHAPTER 4: Miami Dater's Nightmare, Part 1: Connection Stagnation....................................90

CHAPTER 5: Chicago's Not-My-Man Epidemic and the Lesbian Confusion, Parts 1 and 2.........................107

CHAPTER 6: Windy City Fuckboys........................144

CHAPTER 7: Older Men and Dominican Babies: The NYC Scene..171

CHAPTER 8: Miami Dater's Nightmare, Part 2: Come-Out-the-Woodwork Creeps................................203

CHAPTER 9: 34 Times Exhausted........................211

CHAPTER 10: 13 Key Lessons I Learned from 20 Hectic Years of Dating.................................218

CHAPTER 11: Living Single............................234

DEDICATION

This one goes out to all the men I've loved and all the boys who never knew how to love me in return. To the *one* woman who ever made me *really* doubt who I was and the handful of others that awakened something different in me along the way. This book is for all the lovers and the hopers. The cheaters and the cheated. The jaded and the wishful. The hearts wide open and the souls slammed shut. The ones wondering, "Why does this always happen to me?" *and* the ones thinking, "Wow, how did I get this lucky?" It's for those who have felt hurt and those who have done the hurting. For the believers, the non-believers, and the in-betweeners. For the ones who see the future crystal clear and those who still wonder, "Will love ever come for me?"

This is for anyone who has ever believed in love, wanted love, had love, lost love, or forsaken love. I see you, all of you, because, at one point or another, I've *been* you. Life is wild, and love is even wilder. That's what I've learned through it all. And although I've been judged, I won't judge you.

Please know that while most of my stories are written from the perspective of a woman hurt by a man, I don't want the guys to feel like this book isn't for them! Because no matter who you are, I truly believe you can find something to sink your teeth into in these 200 plus pages of pure, unfiltered, human heart.

Thank you for reading.

PREFACE

If I met myself as an adult when I was a kid, a teenager or even a young adult, I wouldn't recognize myself. By the same token, if *she* (a younger, more foolish, or perhaps just less bruised Sonia) met who I am now, her brow would wrinkle defiantly, and she'd scold me with a, "Who are you?" and a look that'd need no words, only flash fire. That's because the all-walls-up cynic that rises from me like a gun from its holster in a moment of doubt each time I start to feel anything at all toward another person is nothing like the lovesick little girl that willingly walked into battle completely unarmed and ready to beg for her life over and over and over again.

Today, still in the midst of this never-ending journey toward love (or perhaps toward nothingness), I find myself battling with my own mind, trying to find a balance between both extremes. Because what's the point of learning so many lessons over the course of almost 20 arduous years of dating if you're not going to use those experiences to do better? But alternatively, what's the point of dating at all if you're just going to shut someone out for every little misstep they take? I pride myself on remaining open to the possibilities, even after everything I've been through in this *novela* (soap opera) I call my love life. But am I *truly* open, or am I just peeking out a tiny little crack in a window that's been continuously lowered slowly and painfully over the years?

I remember it like it was yesterday: my first crushes. Yes, I said crushes, plural. It's that bad—my history of lovesickness—so it's only natural I'd have a plural first crush, right? I was in third grade. They (these two boys) were my friends, and they were always kind to me. Ultimately there was no harm done. I don't think I ever told them how I felt (I was likely too busy trying to figure that out myself), but I remember getting brow-sweat-nervous at the mere sight of them and daydreaming about them when they weren't around. Gross, right?

After my very first crushes, I had a couple of "boyfriends"—relationships defined mostly by sweaty hand-holds, lots of giggling, and a little pop kiss here and there. My first one happened when I was nine years old, and it was sweet, innocent perfection. If only things had remained that simple forever—a girl can dream!

Then sixth grade came, and the sheer level of lovesick grossness skyrocketed to levels that now, in my 30s, seem beyond ridiculous for an 11-year-old. I fell hard for a boy who would go on to torture my young overeager heart for a good five years, give or take. Of course, I played my part in the madness—doing his homework and projects for him (Sonia!), writing poems for him (too deep!), and calling the local radio station (Power Love Hour on Power 96, anyone?) to dedicate songs to him and let him know I loved him (cringe!)—the works.

More on him later, but suffice it to say that was the beginning of a long, tedious, all-consuming ride I couldn't seem to get off of no matter what I did. From crushes, lovers, boyfriends, and one sort-of girlfriend to friends with benefits, a whole lot of obscenely long-winded what-the-heck-are-we-doing-here situationships, and a multitude of unrequited loves, the majority of the decade and a half that followed the sixth grade felt like I was always breaking up with or getting over someone, even though I was technically single for a majority of that time. Talk about all pain, no gain.

And in all that time, man, did I collect some stories and hard-earned lessons. I've done it all and been through it all, and I just know I can't be the only one out there constantly finding herself the butt of the universe's greatest joke when it comes to love. That's why I'm sharing my story in the hopes that I can help you feel less alone, that I can inspire you; comfort you; make you laugh; and, perhaps most of all, help you feel less crazy when you encounter love's sometimes treacherous ways. Because honey, we've all been there at one point or another. Others just ain't going to tell it like it is. But I will. I'll do it with fear in my throat and pain in my chest, but I'll do it, because I feel called to do so.

Here's the good news: Everything I've learned so far has made me undeniably stronger and more confident than I could have ever imagined, and I want to share that power with you. That's the power of knowing who you are, what you want, and what you deserve. It's also the power of patience, because listen, desperation? It smells bad. And I would know—I used to reek of it.

In addition to my dating stories (or as many as I can remember!), I'll also share where I am now as we explore how to find balance in the sometimes long, hurdle-ridden journey toward love. How do we maintain an open heart while still being smart? That, my friends, is the question. Let's see if we can find a middle ground, together.

CHAPTER 1
Heartbreak: The Early Years

Young hearts, not yet jaded, stand freely at the edge, ready to jump overboard for a shiny smile and the promise of love.

His name is, well, not important. Let's call him Mario. Yes. I like that.

Mario and I met in elementary school, and he is my first memory of heartbreak. Sitting here now, writing this, I can't for the life of me remember what I saw in him or how my 11-year-old heart could possibly be that enthralled with another person in the first place; how could I have already been that vulnerable, that desperate for affection?

Mario never had any intentions to do more than get whatever he could from me, but for me, every interaction signaled hope. He called himself my friend, but he never was (this would later emerge as a pattern throughout my life).

There were many nights when I'd finish my homework, put it away, pull out a new sheet of paper, write his name at the very top, and get to work all over again. Even back then I was smart enough to know I had to make the assignment completely different so Mario could get away with it and I could avoid trouble. That part amazes me a little. The rest of it repulses me *a lot*. But hey, I didn't know any better. I thought if I just did what he asked me to, he'd see how great I was, and eventually, he'd want to be my boyfriend. But that never happened. Today I am not at all surprised, but back then, it was a hard blow.

Instead, there were only promises of the gifts he'd get for me or the things he'd do for me in exchange for everything I did for him. And each time I had to sit indignantly in my friend zone and watch him ooze the affection I thought I deserved (and had worked for!), onto a new girlfriend, my young heart would crack just a little more. And at my lowest points, I'd write poems of unrequited love, like the little gem that follows, as an outlet; as a declaration of my pain. (Yes, I've always been a little too deep for my own good!)

I still have the original sheet of paper I wrote it on, complete with smiley faces, scribbles, bad spelling, and *I heart you* doodles—wow! But I'll spare you the horror, and lay it out here, all nice and neat.

Unrequited Love

This unrequited love of mine is making me uneasy.
Sending shivers down my spine, and making me a little dizzy.

Its desperate whispers are driving me up the wall,
shattering my broken heart to pieces.
And soon I think I just might fall.
I'm praying that my heart soon freezes.

I long for the day when my heart will be mine again.
When it will no longer belong to you, and I can break

free from these chains,
for once making happiness come true.

I only ask that you help me ease this pain.
Make him love me or help me break away.
All I ask is that you bring the sun and take away the rain.
Release me from this burden and let my heart once again sing and play.

For I don't know how much longer my heart can endure the suffering that your rejection brings to me.
Or the desperate prayers made along the shore that no one seems to answer.

My prayers continue to be unheard.
My heart continues to break.
I continue to hang onto this thin cord, as my breathe you continue to take.

Amazing and truly frightening all at the same time, huh? And that was just one ill-fated poem. So many more came after that. But that's not the worst part. One day during that sixth-grade year, I had the super bright idea to take my little Tweety Bird–themed tin can filled with sappy love poems for Mario (this is a very real thing that I still have in my possession) to school with me for a reason I can't remember.

Before I knew it, the tin somehow got into the hands of a bully, who proceeded to share my messy, pencil-written poems with everyone and also threatened to keep them—"Finders, keepers," the horrid girl actually said! Now I might have been a little extra in the Feelings Department as a kid, but damn. I'd take that any day over already being as evil as she was at that age. If I close my eyes, I can still see her face smirking at the sheer horror on mine as I tried to wrap my head around what was transpiring.

Mostly I remember being completely flabbergasted at the audacity of this girl to try to ruin my life just for the thrill of it. I can't quite remember how I got my tin back, but I know I put up a fight. It might have involved begging and crying, but hey, I got it back. Nevertheless, the damage had already been done. Everyone now knew my dirty little secret, and Mario, already aware of my ridiculous love for him, now had even more reason to shun me. Although, looking back, it couldn't have been easy to be on his side of this equation either. He must have been (almost) equally embarrassed, and I can appreciate how his own horror might have dictated his behavior from that day forward. I still didn't deserve the way he treated me, but I can see his side of it.

Of course, Mario continued to let me do things for him after that ordeal, but something had shifted. Any respect he might have had for me as a friend had seemingly dissolved into a puddle of embarrassing regret. And for the next few years, we continued to dance our dance, until one day he'd had enough, and he wrote me a note that he delivered at lunchtime in front of all of my friends.

Excited, they thought maybe he'd finally come around and realized his feelings for me, but instead, the note suggested that if I couldn't handle being friends, perhaps we should just end our relationship altogether. I was crushed and probably cried myself to sleep, but I survived. And until I met my first real boyfriend in 11th grade, I continued to pine over Mario—although decidedly more inconspicuously than I had done in the past. My love had turned quiet and tired, but it still burned bright underneath the surface.

I'll never forget how he continued to do things that gave me hope, only to quickly rip it apart. Like when he gifted me a gold ring for my *quinceañera* (the Cuban equivalent to a girl's sweet 16 birthday), but then took a call during the father-daughter dance (#rude!). Luckily or maybe not so much, by then, I had begun to learn to swallow the pain and accept my loveless fate. How tragic for a 15-year-old!

The funny thing, or maybe the even more tragic thing, is that years later, somewhere in my mid-20s, right before I left Miami for Chicago, I *still* hadn't fully learned the extent to which Mario never really cared about me, but only about how good I could make him feel with my blind adoration.

He had just gone through a breakup and decided to reach out to me via Facebook Messenger (oh, how far we had come from the paper notes we'd send each other as kids!). He told me he was sad and lonely, and practically begged me to come over. He just needed a little company, he assured me. He even went as far as to say that I had been the "one who got away." Um. I seem to remember, quite vividly I might add, *you* running away several times bruh, but all right—whatever you say!

I was hesitant to give into his bullshit, but I've always been a sucker for slick words and a broken heart, so I got in my car and drove to him, clutching my heart in my hand, asking myself what the hell I was doing. And from the moment I arrived at Mario's house, something felt very off. I had never so much as kissed Mario in my life, and suddenly, here we were, two adults, alone together in this big house. It didn't help that he had a huge, scary dog (might have even been two, I can't remember exactly) in a crate (I'm over it now, but I used to be deathly afraid of animals!). Mario was a cop, and he said he was training the dog (or dogs) for the force. He was also telling me a lot of strange, aggressive stories about his work that were making me very uncomfortable.

Suddenly, the offbeat vibe penetrating every inch of the atmosphere started to get to me, and my body began to feel very uneasy, but I felt so awkward that I didn't know how to make a smooth exit. So I just sipped nervously at the beer he had offered me and stood awkwardly trying to follow him in conversation.

Abruptly, he started saying things about how much I'd grown up and how much my body had developed since we were kids (well, that's usually what happens, sir). The next thing I knew, he was fairly aggressively touching my butt and jamming his tongue down my throat. (I about died right there! DEAD!) It all felt so wrong (and so good!), but it was also the attention I had been wanting from him for ages (although admittedly a little more rated R than I had ever envisioned as a kid).

My mind raced at what felt like a million miles a second as things continued to escalate. His tongue tasted like validation, and his hands felt like sweet, long-awaited victory. Little by little, the fear and confusion melted away, and I completely gave into him, at which point he suddenly stopped and said, "I can't do this," as I lay on the couch already half naked, my mind swirling from the intensity of the moment.

"What?" I asked, completely and utterly confused.

"I can't do this," he repeated. "You're Sonia. We're friends. I can't use you like this."

Again. "WHAT?!"

I had never jumped to my feet faster than at that moment. I could hardly believe it. This man and his fragile ego had convinced me, against all of my better judgement, to come over and "comfort him" in his time of need. But it all became so clear to me: he just wanted to see if he could still have good ol' lovesick-for-him Sonia. He didn't actually want my friendship or my body, he only wanted to know that he *could* have it. It was his way to boost his confidence after a breakup; to feel that he still had it. I had never been more disgusted by a man in my life (and trust me, even then, that was quite a feat).

Scrambling to pull myself together, I screamed, "I can't fucking believe this shit right now!" as he sat on the couch smirking from ear to ear. I was so angry and nervous that

I struggled to get the front door open. When I finally did, I ran to my car, slammed the door shut, blasted the radio, and punched the steering wheel as I shook my head and kept repeating over and over again, "I can't fucking believe this. I can't fucking believe this." Which I kept up during the entire 20-minute ride back to my apartment that night.

How could I be *so* stupid? How could I let him have that immense satisfaction at the expense of my dignity? How could I forget who he had shown me to be so many times when we were growing up? But alas, I eventually learned to forgive myself and move on.

A few weeks after the incident, I moved to Chicago (a dream come true that had been several years in the making), and it became a little easier to forget. Mario never said a word after I bolted out of his house until another Facebook Messenger alert came a few years later with a too-little-too-late apology that I "accepted" and quickly laughed off.

I never took Mario seriously again, and I was thankful for that. I was finally free of him. And although it took me a good 15 years to get him fully out of my system, he was the beginning of a long journey to self-love—and the heightening of my fuckboy sensors. Most importantly, at that point, I realized that he had never deserved me, and I had certainly never deserved his poison. Today we actually chat here and there, and I really feel no ill will toward him. He is as imperfect as I am, and what happened between us was a long time ago. So I just keep what I learned from him close and handle my interactions with him accordingly.

The biggest lesson I learned from Mario is that sometimes you will like or even love people, and they will not feel the same. There is nothing you can do about such things, and you can't be angry at people for what they feel or don't feel. But not feeling the same about someone as they do about you is no reason to lead them on, lie to them, embarrass them, or use them for your own selfish satisfaction.

Interestingly enough, Mario taught me to be kind in love. And after him, I made it a point to never (consciously) take advantage of someone because they had feelings for me that I did not share. Any time I've found myself in a situation like this, I have tried to be a real friend to the person, be honest with them about how I feel, and respect their heart. That's what I want for myself, and it's what I choose to give to others whenever possible.

I believe this approach lessens the pain, and at the end of the day, makes it so people are better able to accept your feelings in return. Because I can respect a man who doesn't love me, but I can't respect one who punishes me simply for loving him.

And, of course, I've still managed to hurt people along the way. That's inevitable. But I try really hard not to.

Thanks Mario.

CHAPTER 2
Two Boys, One First Love

Everyone is 'the one' when you're young and in love with love.

I was 16 years old and just slipping away from the grip of my obsessive, unrequited love for Mario when I met Diego. I had shared classrooms with him since middle school but had never really noticed him before—not in *that* way, at least. Until this point, he had been the quiet, nerdy guy in the corner desk by the window. Then we started hanging out in the same friend groups, and suddenly my indifference grew into a fiery teenage crush.

We'd joke and laugh and have an amazing time together, but we were just friends. And I knew he had a thing for one of the other girls in the group. She was my friend, but not really. I always knew that girl was triflin' (more on that later!). Anyway, pretty soon I started to sense a more flirtatious vibe from Diego, and so naturally, as any bonafide teenager with a crush would do, I sent someone to ask him who he liked more, my "friend" or me.

His heart-wrenching response? Something to the effect of, "Sonia is really nice, funny, and pretty, but she needs to lose weight." I'll never, ever forget that (even though Diego and I are still friends until this day, and he will surely hate me for mentioning it!). It was my very first taste of weight-saddled rejection. And it's funny, because—yes, I am a thick woman, always have been, and likely always will be—but when I look back at photos of me in high school, I wasn't actually overweight.

I was a size six with thick Cuban thighs and perfectly sized breasts that seemed to suddenly sprout from my previously wall-flat chest the day I turned 13. (In fact, the kids at school used to call me "Skittles" before the great bosom awakening of '97. What a bunch of assholes, am I right?) To boot, I had a big butt, and my face hadn't quite let go of all its delicious baby fat glory.

But to have a 16-year-old boy deem another girl better or more appropriate for a relationship than me because he didn't agree with the size of my body? That was brutal. The worst part is, until that point, I had never even thought of myself as a fat person, or as *just* that. I had always seen myself as pretty, thick, colorful, funny, smart, and kind—basically, a great catch with a fat ass—the very good kind!

But that day, as Diego's thoughtless response made its way back to my eager ears, I realized for the first time, as the weight of the world stood firmly on my shoulders trying to push me into the ground to hide from the embarrassment, how *others* saw me. Still, I picked myself up and, armed with the courage of a computer screen, I confronted Diego about it on AIM (yes—AOL Instant Messenger—it was 2001!).

He told me he didn't say what I had heard, or at least that he hadn't meant it that way. Really, I think he realized that all this Sonia greatness was much bigger than some warped idea of who he thought he should and should not date. Anyway, that conversation ended in a crazy-corny, "Will you be my girlfriend?" ask. And there you had it: I had just embarked on my first (puppy) love. I was over the cheesy teenage moon with my very first legitimate boyfriend!

For the next six months, I couldn't get enough of Diego. I had never liked someone this much who actually liked me in return. What a glorious shift from that salty unrequited love of my preteen years. Walking around holding hands with Diego at school felt like walking on a literal cloud. I always loved school (nerd here!), but I never loved it more than when I was with him. He made me laugh all day long. He made me feel special. He made me feel pretty. He made me feel good.

Diego and I made out all over those halls, to the point where teachers and security guards would yell, "Get a room!" The goodie two-shoes in me was partly horrified, but the so-in-love part of me didn't care. I had never felt more amazing. I even went as far as to stop wearing my beloved lipstick for months so I wouldn't irritate his snow-white-fair skin and not lose out on any of that sweet, delicious lovin' he was doling out like Halloween candy—the good, expensive kind!

And soon enough, shit started to get really real. Before Diego, I had what I self-diagnosed as extreme penis phobia—is that even a real thing? Anyway, I had kissed (tongue included) a couple boys here and there before Diego, but I had been terrified for every minute of those slimy, short-lived lip locks. And the second a boy tried to go anywhere past my lips/face, I would run for the hills or the door or whatever exit was most readily available, sometimes even through just an awkward giggle and a quick change of subject.

At a time when a lot of kids I knew were already experimenting with their bodies, I wasn't ready. In fact, I was beyond unready. Before Diego, the act of making out and all of that just didn't sound or feel appealing to me. Instead, the thought of it filled me with crippling fear. I don't even know why. I had experienced plenty of emotional abuse growing up but never anything physical, other than maybe one boy before Diego who had tried to put his junk on my face while I was sleeping. And, sure, I was grossed out by that, but not traumatized. I was essentially too young to understand it.

Anyway, with Diego, all of those feelings of fear suddenly melted away like a block of ice dissolving on a sultry summer sidewalk. We were in love, and it all just felt so easy, so safe, so comfortable. Nothing felt forced or awkward or gross anymore. In fact, one afternoon, overcome by my affection for him, my phobia completely dissolved as I pressed him against the wall in my bedroom (my dad was very strict about me going out but pretty chill about having boys over—go figure!) and proceeded to do what it do.

I can still see his eyes sort of bulging out of his head in response to my sudden audacity—it was like they were filled with little paper hearts shooting out at me, like something out of a Saturday morning cartoon. Diego always had a way of making everything feel sweet like that. It's probably a big part of how he broke me out of my phobia. I guess you really do catch more flies with honey!

One day, we were fooling around and my hymen broke, and this boy actually went home and researched hymens online. I recall being in this unreal AIM conversation in which he was sending me all kinds of specific scientific information and being extremely concerned that he might have, quite literally, broken me. It was the weirdest and sweetest conversation of my life. And then, a little after that ordeal, on May 7, 2001 (yes, I still remember the date!), just three months short of 17, I went all the way with him, as the kids used to say.

Little did I know that things could get even weirder than that hymen conversation. My first time was quick, strange, and felt incredibly unnatural. I remember texting him, "We're never doing that again!" after his brother picked him up from my house that day. What a hilariously confused couple of kids! Nevertheless, we did do that again (duh), and my love for him only grew each time.

We went to school functions together, and my heart melted just from having him on my arm. I even skipped school and snuck into my house while my dad was out of town to have sex with Diego. Before returning to school, he washed my long, curly hair in the tub (I suffer from a severe case of sexhead) and brushed it all out for me. It's still one of the most romantic (and cheesy) moments I've ever experienced.

When his grandmother passed away just before our two-month anniversary (that's a big deal for a 16-year-old!), he still made sure to have his brother bring him by to give me a heart pendant necklace he had saved up his allowance to buy me (that thing is still at my parent's house somewhere!). More than anything, we shared a lot of laughter and so much love.

But inevitably, our rosy love also had its thorns. As I mentioned, my dad was pretty strict about me going out, and Diego's parents didn't even let him have a girlfriend at the time. So we'd have to plan, scheme, and sneak around, finding creative ways to have our dates and time together. Summer was a particularly hard time; we were out of school and lost our most accessible and frequent hangout spot.

There was also the issue of money. I was 16, working 20-plus hours a week, and excelling in honors and advanced-placement courses in school, as well as other extracurricular activities. My parents didn't have much money, and I liked being able to pay for my own things with what I earned from my job. I also enjoyed the freedom that working gave me. But Diego didn't have a job and wasn't a particularly good student either (sorry boo!).

Often I paid for our dates and for his lunch at school, and that was frustrating to me. Many times it ruined the mood and caused fights between us. Here I was, 16, and arguing about money with my boyfriend. It just didn't feel right. Why was I on free/reduced lunch but paying for this boy's pizza?

I'll never forget how I lost it one day when we went on a dinner date and he ordered a $30 fish at a Thai restaurant. He just didn't understand. He was also 17, and I get that. But it was still infuriating when I thought of the aching feet of standing at my job for hours on end and the sleepless nights of studying that it took for me to be able to earn that money and keep my grades up.

But even aside from the money, things just became too hard between us. So one night in late summer, over the phone, after six months together, with tears in our eyes and knots in our throats, we decided to end it.

The weeks that followed were excruciating. I thought Mario had broken my heart before, but I had never felt the pain of breaking up with someone who actually loved me back. Of letting go of a relationship not because feelings had died but because logistics had become too difficult, to the point where it was almost out of our hands. I guess that's just what tends to happen when a couple of kids fall in love.

I couldn't eat. My mom would bring me food, and I'd throw it in the trash and cover it with paper towels in the hopes that she wouldn't realize. I couldn't sleep either. All I could manage to do was lay around, cry, and listen to Shakira's *Laundry Service* album over and over and over again.

I lost 10 pounds in those two weeks before my senior year in high school (bright side!). That's truly the one time in my life that sadness or depression has taken away my appetite instead of giving me a ferocious, insatiable one. That's first love for you!

In late August 2001, I strutted back into school, ready to face Diego and everyone for the first time since the breakup. To my surprise, I was in three classes with him. Mind you, prior to this, I had never been in so much as one class with him during all of high school. To make matters worse, it wasn't only him in those three classes.

Remember that "friend" who was in the running before he "chose" me? She was there too, and very soon, she became his new girlfriend. I sat in those classes with one hand covering the side of my face closest to them so they couldn't see the tears streaming down, quietly but heavily, as I listened to them laugh, play, and carry on.

How could he move on *that* fast while I was still dying inside? But eventually, after all the tears; bargaining; and silly, petty attempts at making him jealous subsided, as these things usually do, I too moved on. Or so I thought. More on that later.

Over the course of the next decade plus, Diego and I remained friends, although he would mostly come around in-between girlfriends. And I, being the forever single girl, was always there to welcome him with open arms. He made it easy. We had a great time together, and he could effortlessly make me laugh. He also remained one of the nicest guys I had ever known, and he never made me feel bad. Instead he lifted me up.

Our friendship was complicated, swinging consistently somewhere in-between just friends and we'll-always-be-just-a-little-bit-more. We continued to flirt and sleep together throughout the years, and even though I never stopped loving him and being around him, I felt that we had grown up to be two very different people, so I would never truly be happy with him if we decided to take it any further.

One evening, when I was visiting Miami from Chicago and he picked me up from the airport, we went to a bar where, after a couple of drinks, he started to tell me how much he loved me. I told him I loved him too. It's something we often communicated. But he insisted, "I *love* you, love you, like I would marry you love you." I didn't know what to say, and I knew in my heart, despite the fact that he was a perfectly wonderful man, that he was not the one for me. So I just awkwardly giggled and leaned in for a hug. I think he got the point.

Soon after that encounter and our final sexual rendezvous during a subsequent visit to Chicago, Diego would meet the woman he is now happily married to, and even though it was inevitable, I really struggled to let him go. He had been a constant in my life for a long time, more than 15 years, and since we were very young. He was consistently kind and always had my back. In my life, I had known few men who were as decent as him or cared about me in the way that he did. He was my backup (you know, that person you could be OK ending up with if you never met anyone else you'd want to marry). But that's the thing about backups. They eventually move on—without you.

I cried my eyes out like a baby in the weeks before Diego's wedding, which I was not invited to, even though we never stopped being close. I had never met his fiancé, now wife, and I guess it would have been too awkward to introduce me for the first time as a wedding guest. It just proved to me once and for all that we would forever be a little more than friends—otherwise, I would have been there. I remember sitting in the movie theater in New York City by myself on the Monday night before the wedding watching *My Big Fat Greek Wedding 2*, sobbing and thinking of him and his impending nuptials.

Sometimes you just need to ball up all of those confusing emotions and cry them out! I also made sure to get myself on a bus to Washington, D.C., the weekend of his wedding, where I had a lot more friends than I did in New York and would be more entertained while it was all going down.

At the time, I couldn't even comprehend (and my friends understood it even less) why I felt so deeply hurt, when I knew I didn't really want to be with or marry Diego. I think it was more about knowing that this backup I had for so many years, this cute boy who could always make me feel good, was going to be out of my life for good.

Marriage obviously changes things, and we rarely talk anymore. But that's just the way life goes, and after missing him pretty intensely for a long time, I'm finally totally at peace with essentially losing my friend. A friendship like ours couldn't respectfully go on because there was always a deep history at play in our interactions and a less-than-subtle flirtation there to contend with, too. But it's OK. It's been hard but also completely necessary to fall back a bit. And the good thing is, I think we will always be on good terms. Friends from a distance with nothing but love and appreciation between us which is something that I can't say I've had with any other ex of mine.

Thank you Diego for the many years of love and friendship we shared and for giving me an example of what a good man is, even on my most pessimistic days. I appreciate you, and I miss you! I'm also happy you're happy. Seriously dude. Good for you!

A second chance at first love

A few months after my breakup with Diego, I met Luca through a friend whose boyfriend worked with him as a lifeguard at the local water park. She knew I was a complete mess over Diego and thought setting me up might help. And it did—for the time being.

So she put us in contact (he went to a different high school), and he agreed to meet me at the grocery store where I worked after school. I was manning the express lane at the far-right end of the store when he came through the line with a huge bag of Funyuns; a big, goofy smile; and a twinkle in his eye that let me know this was the famous Luca my friend had sent to meet me. "Damn, he's fine!" I thought as I caught his eye for the very first time.

I checked him out and told him what time I'd be on my break. He waited around a bit, and once my break came, I grabbed a snack and sat with him on a bench at the front of the store. We chatted for a bit and instantly hit it off. Although how hard is it to hit it off with a sexy, friend-recommended stranger at 17 on the heels of a gut-wrenching breakup? Not very!

After our initial meeting, we decided to plan a proper first date, which took some creativity, because I wasn't allowed to go out with a boy like that, even at 17, and even if the guy had signed away his left kidney to my dad as promise of my safe return. So I told my dad I was hanging out at a friend's house, and Luca and I went off on a double date with the friend who hooked us up and her boyfriend.

I can't believe the kind of guts I used to have for that sort of big ol' lie! These days, I'm a terrible, terrible liar. I guess you give a young girl no other choice, and she will do what she has to do. Especially when it comes to a cute boy and the promise of a new love.

I wore a pair of blue satin-y capris with a light and dark blue striped shirt; wedges; and my crazy long, curly, and almost-blonde hair pinned up to the sides. And, of course, I couldn't forget my shiny pink lipstick. Feeling like a million and one bucks, I headed off with the others to Bayside, a marketplace by the water in downtown Miami.

Luca looked and smelled good (no, great!), he opened doors, and he paid. I was in teenage date heaven. And, well, that's all it really took in those days. Pretty soon after that date, Luca and I were boyfriend and girlfriend. I was still in love with Diego, but if I had to find a way to get over him, this wasn't a bad way to go about it. Did I mention how gorgeous Luca was?

It also helped that my dad loved him. While Diego's parents were weird about letting him come over to my house and had zero interest in even meeting me, Luca's parents wanted to get to know me, and my dad equated that with respect. Luca was also allowed to do pretty much whatever he wanted, and he had a car, so visits and outings were much easier to finagle. Yes, Luca would still have to park his car at our house so my dad could then take us wherever we were going, but we found our way around the rules nonetheless.

At first, as things intensified between Luca and me, they were also a little rocky. You see, I was Luca's first everything, and he was only my close second. Don't get me wrong; I was super into him, and we were having a lot of fun together. But at the time, he could never replace what I had felt for Diego and all the firsts we had experienced together. Luca wanted so badly for me to love him at the same pace and level as he did me, but I told him he would have to give me time. I knew I'd get there, I was just on a different journey. And soon, sure enough, I fell just as hard as he had. Life seemed to be on fire with the spark between us.

We were still kids, and sometimes our love got us into trouble. One night after a club banquet at school, we came back to my house and hung out in my room as we usually did. Strangely enough, my dad rarely bothered us, so we got over-confident that day. Lo and behold, my older sister was visiting from college for the weekend and had gone out somewhere without telling my dad. So he came to my bedroom looking for her.

Just five minutes before that, Luca had been egging me on to undress, to which I suggested we just do our usual, much safer, sneaky-teenager-friendly clothes-on sexual extravaganza. But damn, he looked so good, and the charm was spilling from his mouth and eyes like icing from a piping gun. So I gave in, and as my dad walked in with *no* warning, I wanted the ground to open up and swallow my naked body so I could escape the sheer horror of that moment.

It's a bit of a blur; I remember running to the in-room bathroom, almost slipping on the floor to face my untimely demise, and making up some story about having a big stomachache. Yes, somehow my horrified 17-year-old brain thought that faking a painful bowel movement was my best out from this obvious charade.

As Luca was leaving (he thankfully remained fully clothed the entire time), I think my dad was too in shock to yell at anyone (I had always been a good kid, but alas, teenagers will be teenagers), so Luca escaped untouched.

The next day Luca came by, spoke to my dad, and apologized. To my surprise, Luca's apology was accepted, and he was allowed to keep coming over, so long as we stayed downstairs and didn't go up to my bedroom. The funny part is that my dad, trusting we wouldn't do anything outside the comfort of a more private bedroom, would go to sleep and leave us to "watch movies" on the couch. It was the easiest, least nerve-racking sex of our young lives. Poor dad.

And I was such a good kid that my punishment the day after we were caught was to stay home from school and from work. WHAT? Luckily, these unfortunate set of events came about a week before my dad was set to leave for a trip to Cuba, and by the time he got back, he had either forgotten or chosen to forget.

Also luckily for me, my dad's trip coincided with my senior prom, which I likely would not have been allowed to go to had he been around. His absence allowed Luca and me to go all out. My mom was definitely not the strict one in our house.

I don't think I've ever felt as beautiful as I did that night in my sparkly peach-pink, diamond neckline, tube top, floor-length gown that I had bought for myself with my part-time job money. I also splurged for hair, nails, and makeup, and a group of friends and I went in on a limo to get us to the party. I felt so fancy! And my happiness glow was only heightened by the tall, dark, and handsome arm candy I had that night and the fact that I finally got to show him off to Diego and his new girlfriend. Because Luca didn't go to my high school, this would be the first time most of my friends would get to meet him too.

I distinctly remember Diego making animal noises any time we'd pass by him at the dance. It seemed like a bizarre way to signal jealousy, but all right. Diego had never been a cruel guy, so I know he must have been out of his mind with envy to behave that way. That's OK. I basked in the joy of it all and laughed off his antics. I had never felt so powerful in my young life.

I stayed out until 4:00 a.m. that night, which was unheard of for me. Even 10:00 p.m. was a struggle when my dad was around. After the prom, a couple of us went to get some late-night pizza, and then I went back to Luca's house with him. His parents were not strict with him at all—he could legitimately do as he pleased. (They definitely sang a different tune when it came to his sister though—it was that Cuban family double standard hard at work!)

When I think about it now, that night left me feeling a little empty. It almost felt *too* grown up and free, and I wasn't sure what to do with it. Maybe part of me was in over my head. Or maybe my heart was still not fully present with Luca but remained a few months back with Diego. That's the thing about revenge, or whatever you want to call it. Sometimes after you finally get to taste it, it doesn't fill you up nearly as much as you had anticipated. But on I went with Luca, and in time, I fell more and more in love with him and, eventually, out of love with Diego.

Pretty soon it was time to head off to college at the University of Florida, and I left Luca behind in Miami, although we would still date on and off for a while—perhaps for too long a while. The day I left, he came by the house to say goodbye, and I thought I might actually collapse and die from how hard it was. I cried for him for maybe the first two weeks at my new home in Gainesville, and after that things got easier and harder all at the same time.

College immediately opened up a whole new world to me, and I had the kind of balls-to-the-wall freedom I had never even had a taste of growing up with a strict dad. I was doing whatever I wanted whenever I pleased—meeting new people and running my own show. And my God, it felt completely, almost overwhelmingly, amazing. Suddenly this whole boyfriend thing didn't feel as magical or as life-affirming as it once did. Mostly it just felt like an obstacle, but I did love Luca, and I was trying as hard as I could to make it work.

By the end of that summer, I didn't have it in me anymore, and I broke up with Luca at the end of one of his visits. He wasn't scheduled to drive back to Miami until later that day, but the moment I opened my mouth, he had tears in his eyes and his duffel bag in his hand, ready to jet out the door. It was so sad. I've never been able to deal with seeing a man cry, maybe because I had seen so little of it in my life. And he wasn't just teary eyed. He was full on blubbering. It broke my damn heart in two, but it still didn't change my mind. I was young, and I had finally tasted freedom. I wasn't ready to give that up for a boy.

As Luca drove off, I began blubbering too, and as soon as I got back to my dorm from that pain-struck parking lot, I fell into my bed, doubting what I had just done. Not long after, I went to Miami for a weekend and saw him. Those same tears that had welled up in his eyes, glistening with pain the moment I broke up with him a few weeks prior, seemed to have taken residence there. And soon I felt compelled to give things another chance. Not because I wanted to reenter a relationship, but because I thought, "Wow, he must really love me. How can I walk away from that?"

It's funny how we rationalize our choices when we're young, thinking someone's feelings for us are enough to sustain our own. Heck, there are still times when I do this in moments of weakness and insecurity, but never quite so freely or as unquestioned as I did that day. And it wouldn't take long at all before I would began to regret my choice.

Luca had always been a simple guy and a jealous guy. He didn't have a lot of friends—well, barely any, really. At 17 and 18, he preferred to stay home and watch TV rather than go out and have any kind of experience. Having dealt with that kind of who-needs-experiences-or-friends-to-be-happy attitude from my family all of my life, this was always a big issue for me. He even used to say I had too many friends and that friendship only brought problems. Maybe he was partially right, but who wants to miss out on life like that in fear of getting hurt? Not me! Especially not then.

Luca didn't like that I was away at college. He didn't like it when I went out or met new people, and he certainly didn't like it when I drank or did pretty much anything that required me to leave the house or talk to anyone else other than him. He didn't even like it when I studied. Legitimately—the man was jealous of my books. Often he'd call me, and when I told him I'd talk to him later because I needed to study or do homework, he would get super angry and call me repeatedly until I was forced to talk to him. He would do the same thing if he knew I was trying to take a nap.

His favorite line was, "If you love me, you would..." Everything was based on conditions, and every move I made was a reason to question my intentions. I would often say Luca was my dad in a young man's body, to which he would angrily reply, "I'm not your dad!" But oh, he was. In so many ways he was, and at that time in my life and in my journey, that wasn't a good thing.

So I rebelled, and I cheated. Luca's pushing, questioning, and controlling doesn't justify my actions, but he quickly drove me to abandon any sense of right and wrong, which at 18 and newly freed into the welcoming arms of a raging college town, was almost too easy. It was the perfect weekend to lose control too—the University of Florida vs. University of Miami football game—and the streets were lit with possibility.

I met Jorge at a house party. He was cute, sweet, gentle, and fun. And at that moment, he was everything I needed to forget about my maddening boyfriend back in Miami. "You want to control me so badly?" I thought with my childish, drunken brain. "I'll show you!" So that night, I let Jorge take me by the hand and bring me home. And the moment my eyes shot open the next morning, still in his deceit-laced bed, I felt my heart sink down to my stomach as my stomach sank down to my toes.

I walked home to my dorm that morning wondering what the heck I had just done and what I would say to Luca. Like I said, I wasn't usually a good liar, and this one would really test me. But I couldn't bare the truth, and so, in one of my most shameful moments of mental fog to date, I decided to tell him that I had fallen asleep at a party after drinking too much and awoke with a man inside of me.

It's throat-closing-difficult to write that even now, so many years later. How awful to make something like that up, something that no doubt actually happened to many young women in college, something that placed such ugly blame on another (although I didn't use any names or falsely incriminate anyone), simply because I was too much of a coward to place it on myself, where it belonged. I'm truly sorry for that. But in that moment, it's what I did. And until this day, there is little I've done or said in my life that I'm more ashamed of than what I did in that moment.

Luca was devastated, and mad at himself that he couldn't be there to protect me, which made my treacherous lie that much more awful. So it wasn't long before I found myself calling him to tell him the truth. First he went silent, and then a ton of screaming and insults shot at me like grenades. I sat there and took it, tears running down my red-hot face. There was nothing else for me to do. I would have likely done the same had the tables been turned. Eventually he hung up on me, and I remained where I sat, somewhere on campus, in shock and unsure of what to do next.

The next couple of weeks involved a whole lot of groveling and bargaining, and it was *ugly*. I don't remember many details, except that I begged him to let me come see him in Miami for Valentine's Day so I could prove how sorry I was and how much I loved him. (GROSS). I asked, "If I show up at your door Friday night, will you open it?" He said, "maybe," and so off I went.

I didn't have a car, so I took the bus to Walmart and bought a bunch of stuff for a special, romantic picnic I was planning. That was quite the arduous little trek! I got heart-decorated plates and cups, a red table cloth, candles and candle holders, a frame for a collage I had made him with pictures of us, and a poem I had written him in the center of it all. (This is what I do, people. If I love you, I write poems for you!) This would end up being the centerpiece for our romantic indoor picnic. I even got some lingerie, which I'm not sure I had ever done before or was even prepared for, but I was *that* desperate to prove my love.

I also got my very first tattoo: a "tramp stamp" with two Precious Moments (does that take you back or what?!) angels kneeling, getting married. I had the tattoo artist make the boy's hair brown like Luca's and the girl's blonde, like mine was at the time. And every second hurt like pure, fiery hell! In my very unwise 18-year-old mind, I thought if I subjected myself to some semblance of the level of pain that I caused him, Luca might see how sorry I was and ultimately take me back.

Even though I went to Miami that weekend, got him to open the door, and eventually convinced him to take me back, it was the beginning of a painful, embarrassing charade that would go on for nearly two more years. It wasn't until he ended up doing something awful to me that I finally got it through my thick, lovesick, guilt-riddled head that he really didn't care about me anymore and he never would. He would always be angry with me, and although I had fucked up royally, I could not and would not spend my entire life begging for his forgiveness and letting him treat me like garbage.

But first, here are the gruesome details of the pitifully hopeful, and now clearly tragic, Valentine's show I put on for him. Luca still lived with his parents at the time, so I convinced his sister to let me use her apartment (which was attached to the house his parents and he lived in, but private) to make him an elaborate meal and have an adult romantic night that wouldn't exactly work in the confines of his bedroom. (I've never been much of a cook, so this was a big deal!)

I had printed out a recipe for chicken parmesan back at school, and his sister took me shopping for the ingredients while he was at work (there's no way I hauled chicken from that Walmart in Gainesville all the way to Miami and lived to tell about it!). Once the meal was complete, I took a shower, got all gussied up, and set my romantic picnic up in the living room. Eventually, I'd bring out that lingerie too—blush!

My whole heart was spread out on the cheesy picnic blanket that night, and although Luca mostly played along, I still felt his anger and disgust gurgling up underneath his smile like bubbly foam spilling from a broken washer. And the sex was far from the get-our-love-back-on-track fantasy I had created in my head. Instead it felt mechanical, forced, and dry. He nitpicked the food, the setup, and the tattoo I had gotten for him—he even criticized the lingerie. He also felt the need to tell me that he had planned to propose before everything went down, but I had ruined everything. Why even tell me that? But I guess I deserved it. Sigh.

Nevertheless I continued to swallow my pride and smile through it all, because after what I had done, I felt like I deserved the treatment. It was a small price to pay for his forgiveness. And it would all eventually become the pattern of our ultimate and permanent demise.

I don't remember the rest of that weekend, but I'm sure it was full of the same pretenses and sad, disguised rejection of that Valentine's night. Still, I got on the bus back to Gainesville on Sunday, somehow filled with hope that everything would be OK in due time. But just a few days later, I got a call from Luca during which he said, this time without cover or pretense, "I don't love you anymore." It felt like I had been stoned right through the phone. We hung up. Then I yelled, cried, and threw the big teddy bear (sorry, Hughey!) he had given me on our two-month anniversary across the room.

I felt defeated and embarrassed, naive and broken. But although his delivery was cruel, he was acting out of pain; pain that I had caused. So I accepted my fate. It still, however, didn't stop me from contacting him every time I went to Miami, and even when I wouldn't be in town, every couple weeks, just to check on him. I had this incessant need to hear his voice and know he was OK. Even if he could no longer feel love for me, my love for him had never been more intense. Sure, I was dating plenty of men back at college, but my heart was always with Luca in Miami.

The worst part is he was never kind to me again, even when he tried to be. But still I'd call and beg, and he'd let me come see him. Mostly we would hook up, but here and there we'd catch a movie or grab a meal; maybe even engage in a quick, mediocre cuddle that always felt as if it was being timed, like cupcakes baking in the oven. It wasn't much, but I couldn't let go, and I was always prepared to accept whatever measly crumbs he was willing to offer. Even several years after the whole cheating debacle, my ever-fragile self-esteem continued to believe that this is what I deserved forever because of that one night and mistake I had made at 18.

Fortunately or unfortunately, the night would eventually come when I'd finally learn that I didn't have to continue to accept this never-ending punishment. During one of the most awful moments of my life to date, something in my mind finally clicked. And even though I obviously wish it hadn't taken something so extreme to finally help me let go of Luca forever, I am grateful it ended there and not another couple of years later.

I'm talking about the night that Luca raped me (wow it's difficult to type that word even today, but it's my truth—*the* truth.). For a long time after it happened, I felt like I didn't have the right to the word rape. It happened in his house, in his bedroom, on the same bed we had shared consensually dozens, maybe even hundreds, of times before. I even felt like I had somehow instigated what had happened.

Here's how that night went down.

Luca and I were lying in bed watching a movie, when he started throwing a fit about my not wanting to have anal sex with him. We had made the attempt a few other times, but it just wasn't fun for me. More than that, it always hurt like hell, even through our clumsy not-all-the-way trials, and I couldn't for the life of me figure out how people could possibly find this pleasurable. Do you, folks, but I cannot!

I tried to explain this to him during his childlike tantrum—the likes of which today, I would have undoubtedly walked out on, but was not yet quite strong or aware enough to do back then. I said that I was by no means trying to deprive him of any pleasure or be prude (which would have been my right, anyway!). I simply didn't enjoy it and would prefer to do our thing the traditional way.

But alas, that was not enough for Luca, and he continued to kick, scream, and pout until I just about lost my mind. So I made him a deal. If he would let me insert a skinny little pen (nothing compared to his plans) into his own backside and be OK, I would let him try anal again with me. I was attempting to show him just a fraction of the discomfort that he was begging to put me through. To my surprise, he actually agreed, and so in the pen went for probably no more than a second or two.

I am a woman of my word, so I kept my promise and let him have another try at the whole backdoor fiasco. I insisted that we were simply making an attempt and had him promise he would stop and exit if I became too uncomfortable. He agreed, but he lied.

After a few fumbly tries, he made his way all the way in, at which point I immediately felt unbearable pain and started screaming, "No, no, no. Get out! Get out!" as I tried to simultaneously push his body off mine. Instead of taking my screams, pushing, and direct "no"s as his cue to stop, he jammed his tongue down my throat with the power of a garden hose at full blast to drown out my screams; to drown out my *voice.*

I felt my body go limp as the pressure of his body became too much for me to fend off. There was nothing left to do but let it happen and wait for it to end. He pounded and pounded until he was finished, until he was satisfied, and only then was I free. With my face drenched in tears, my throat sore from fighting, my body folding into itself like spaghetti, and my mind in shock from what the last 10 minutes (that felt like hours) had been, I gathered my clothes, maybe managed to mutter a word or two, and left.

At first, and for a long time after, I didn't tell anyone about what happened, and if you haven't already noticed, I'm not one to keep a big life story (or even a small one) to myself. But this was different. I was confused and ashamed, and at the time, I thought I had instigated the whole ordeal with my now-clearly-ridiculous butt pen trial.

I also wasn't sure what it meant that this was a person I knew intimately and had slept with willingly many times before that night. This hadn't happened to me at the hands of a stranger in some dark alley. It had happened in a bedroom I walked into voluntarily that time and 100 times before that. And it had happened after I had consented to trying, even though I had asked that he stop if I became too uncomfortable. But that nuance, at that time, still didn't make me feel confident in my feelings that I had been raped.

So I didn't talk about it. Instead I let the story out abruptly to unsuspecting friends and bystanders after a few drinks. Mostly it would come out in incoherent tear-stained babbles, so I'm not sure anyone even really understood what I was saying. While sober, there were little triggers everywhere like anytime someone mentioned or joked about anything and everything butt-related, but every time my eyes welled up, I breathed deeply and forced my eyes to swallow back the pain.

After that night I found the strength to walk away from Luca once and for all. I quit him cold turkey. I stopped calling him to check in. I stopped letting him know when I would be in Miami. I just stopped. For better or for worse, what had transpired had finally made me break those chains and walk away from a situation that had been self-imploding for a long time.

Then, one day, maybe four months or so after the rape, Luca called me. He asked where I had been and if I had stopped reaching out because I had a new boyfriend. No boyfriend, I told him.

Then I asked, "You really have no idea why, after chasing you forever, I would walk away and never contact you again, just like that?"

He said he had no idea, so I reminded him of what happened that night. That's when he proceeded to call me a "psycho" who needed to go to therapy.

"Is that what you're telling people? That I'm a rapist?" he said, almost laughing.

I don't remember how the conversation ended, but after that we never spoke again.

We did, however, have a couple of run-ins once I moved back home to Miami after college. I found out that, just a few short months after things between us had ended for good (after the rape), Luca met a girl and got her pregnant. As far as I'm aware, they're still together today, and I wish them the best. Even before the rape, when things were not quite so tragic between us, Luca could have never been the man for me in the long-run.

He wanted me to quit college, come home, and have his babies—all at 18 years old (he actually gave me this exact ultimatum once–come home to be with him or break up—and it caused one of our plentiful breakups). He wanted me to be a homebody and not have "too many" friends, or any at all, really. Ideally I would be quiet and meek and little more than his possession. And if he found what he wanted somewhere else, and she could genuinely be happy with a man like that, then more power to them. But that's definitely a big, flaming, "no, thank you!" from me.

The funny thing is, this girl always kept an eye on me, even though there has never been even an inch of a reason to do so. The few times I ran into Luca in Miami, he was usually with her. And every time my knees would buckle, he would get a look on his face like he'd seen a ghost, and I would quickly leave or peel off in my car. Basically, I would just get away as fast as I could.

I guess she would take both of our reactions as indication that there was still something there, but there wasn't—just a lot of history and even more pain. One time she even sent me a MySpace (yes, MySpace!) message telling me to stay away from her man. I laughed and felt a little sorry for her.

Even as recently as 2016, after running into him in a Walgreens parking lot, I received a quick like/unlike from her on one of my Instagram pictures—watch those fingers, honey! It boggles my mind that he would run into me and then tell her, but I imagine that's why she looked me up after all this time.

Anyway, it did take me a good six or seven years to truly get over Luca and everything that had gone on between us, but I always dealt with that pain by myself—I never went to him for relief from it as I have often done with others after him. Maybe I knew how unsafe and unproductive that would inevitably be.

Once, after a few of these Miami run-ins, I went to see a psychic (yes, I believe in psychics, and I also totally understand if you don't). He told me he saw a man from my past who now had a wife and a young baby but could not get me out of his head. The psychic also said this man had finally realized what he had done wrong, and he couldn't stop kicking himself for it. That's when I began to *bawl*.

The physic tried to comfort me by saying in Spanish, "It's OK. Don't cry. He is not the man for you." I told him I wasn't crying tears of pain but tears of joy. I always knew full well that Luca hadn't woken up the morning he raped me and thought, "Hmm, I think I'll assault Sonia today." Instead, I know it was a moment that escalated, during which he made a terrible choice.

That doesn't make it right or excusable, but knowing that it wasn't a planned attack did make healing a little easier for my mind and heart. Hearing that he had finally realized what he did and that he was sorry for it, even if it came from a psychic's mouth and not his own, brought me a great deal of relief. That's all I had ever wanted—him recognizing what he had done and apologizing for it. And during that visit with the psychic, I felt I got both. It was also the same moment in which my journey to truly getting past what had happened and over Luca in general began.

Although I never spoke to him again, he's always somewhere in the back of my mind, even to this day. I often joke to myself, "If I had known he would be the last real boyfriend I'd ever have, I might have put up with a little more bullshit." But in all honesty, no matter the cost, I'm forever grateful I walked away from that kind of present *and* future.

Thank you Luca for teaching me to love myself above all else, even when it tears my heart out a little (or a lot) to do so. It still brings me a great deal of pride that, even at just 18 years old, when you asked me to choose between you and my education, my future, I had enough foresight and self-love to choose myself before a boy. Because what would have been the point of holding on to love (and unhealthy love, at that) if it meant losing myself?

CHAPTER 3
Looking for Love in *All* the Places:
The College Years

Sometimes looking for love looks a whole lot like clawing for attention.

Once I started to let go of Luca and work through my related trauma, I was unstoppable on the collegiate dating scene. To be honest, I was wild even when Luca was still in the picture, since at that point we were just two exes who spoke and saw each other once in a while. But I digress.

My standards weren't exactly properly formed at that point, so if someone was cute and DTF (down to fuck), I was game. All I wanted was to be as free as a bird and have fun. I had gone from the strictness of my father to an overbearing boyfriend, and I just wanted to do whatever the hell I felt like for as long as I possibly could. And at that age, for better or for worse, that usually involved late nights of dancing my heart out and cute (although sometimes not so cute) boys.

I reveled in the attention and the freedom, and for a while, I reveled hard. There were even times when I would go to lunch with one guy in the afternoon and meet up for "dessert" with another that same evening. And why not? I was young, free, and always safe. Plus I made sure to be open about what I was doing; I never hid my promiscuity or intentions from anyone, and I wasn't committed to anyone in particular, either.

My wild stage continued until the end of sophomore year. I slept around so long as I was having fun and owning it. The minute I had gotten it out of my system, and it was no longer fun or fulfilling, I pulled back. I didn't become a saint of any sort, just a little pickier with my time and my bed.

And in the course of those five and a half years (four in undergrad and one and a half in grad school), I even managed to fall in love and get my heart broken a few times. There were *a lot* of guys back in those days, many whose names I couldn't tell you today. To be honest, I probably couldn't even pick most of 'em out of a lineup, but inevitably there were a few that played a bigger role and made a little dent: Mackenson, Andrew, and Tafari.

My First Taste of Haiti

I met Mackenson when I was still in high school and had gone to Gainesville to visit my sister, but nothing more than dancing happened between us until I was about 19 and in my second year at University of Florida. I met him for the first time at a party in a club. And even though I don't remember all the details of that night, I totally remember what I was wearing. If I close my eyes, I can picture the entire outfit from head to toe, accessorized by my then waist-long curls and the deep naiveté of a young girl who had barely left her neighborhood before, much less her entire city and environment.

I wasn't into Mackenson at first (and I was still dating Luca, too), but I was always intrigued by him. At the time, I had never heard a smooth, beautiful French accent or tasted milk-chocolate lips like his. His Haitian hips naturally swayed with my Cuban soles, and his desire for me brimmed in his little beady, eager eyes from the moment he set his sights on me.

We kept in touch a little throughout my last year of high school before I moved to Gainesville for school, and once I got there, he was just as eager to see me as the day we met. For about a year or so after I moved, Mackenson was nothing more than a friend. I didn't have a car, and he would offer to drive me wherever I needed, at times even picking me up from a nightclub at one in the morning if I was ready to go home before my friends were.

No matter what I was doing or where I was, I could always count on him to be there for me. And, sure, his ulterior motives were always there, but I still considered him a good friend. That probably had a lot to do with the fact that he never made any physical moves on me or made me feel uncomfortable. He just seemed happy to be around me and spend time together. Maybe he was working me the whole time, and if he was, eventually, he succeeded.

The next year, on his birthday, I decided I was ready to be more than just friends, so I basically said, "OK, I'm ready. Happy birthday!" How humble of me, right? He was in absolute shock but immediately jumped at the offer. And although the chemistry we had built over time was pretty explosive, I could have done without all the talking that happened after I gave him the greenlight. He must have said, "You have no idea how long I've wanted this," and "I've waited so long for this" about five or six times in the span of one hour. Not knowing what to say, and feeling the pressure of it all literally on top of me, I just smiled and tried not to die of embarrassment.

After that night, Mackenson and I dated and messed around on and off for about eight years. But we were never on the same page. When he was ready to be mine, I wasn't ready to be his, and when I was finally ready to be his, he no longer wanted the commitment. Still, we danced. Entire semesters passed during which we would sleep (yes, actually sleep) together every night and pretty much be a couple. Then there were other times when we weren't as consistent but still reached out and saw each other often. We held hands and enjoyed birthday dinners together. But we never once called each other boyfriend and girlfriend.

At the end of one of our final stretches when we were hanging out consistently and I was ready to commit, as we laid in bed together, I asked Mackenson to make it official. Suddenly, he looked very uncomfortable, but he tried to be kind. That's when he told me he wasn't really looking for a girlfriend because he'd be graduating soon and leaving Gainesville (he was a few years older than me).

He also said that our time had passed, and although he cared about me a lot, he just wasn't there anymore as far as wanting to commit after waiting for my feelings to catch up to his for so long. It was an open and honest (or so I thought at that moment) conversation, and I appreciated the way he handled it. I was still sad and cried, but I couldn't be angry.

That is, of course, until a short time later, when I found out that he had taken a girlfriend. To make things even worse, this was a girl who had already managed to date my ex Diego and allegedly my sort-of ex Andrew (more on him later). She also lived with some friends of mine, including my first girl crush (more on her later, too). Oh, the tangled webs we weave!

Anyway, that really wasn't the worst part, even though he had *just* finished telling me he wasn't looking to commit to anyone. But soon enough he was knocking on my door telling me he had only agreed to be her boyfriend because she wouldn't sleep with him otherwise. Well, OK. That's depressing!

Here's my thing. Obviously, at least in some instances, that strategy works, but why in the hell would I ever want to force (or coerce) someone into being with me by using my anatomy as a weapon or bargaining tool? Maybe it plays a part in why I'm still single till this day, but I just cannot with the childish, manipulative games. I'd frankly rather die alone.

Big surprise: Mackenson ended up cheating on this forced-upon-him girlfriend with me, and my ego was *too* big to say no. I felt like he was mine to have after all of our history. (This was definitely a recurring issue for me. Eventually I got my shit together.)

Then came the very worst part, when I received an email, with the subject line something to the tune of "Mackenson: The E! True Hollywood Story," from this girlfriend, who had discovered that he was not only messing with both of us at the same time but also had a girlfriend in Haiti the entire time she and I had known him.

There were date-stamped photos of him with his Haitian girlfriend in Gainesville—you know, the kind people used to print before smartphones and digital everything. I was shocked, to say the least. I had *no* idea. None. All those years I had spent being either friends or more with Mackenson, I never once suspected anything. He was *that* good.

I think that was the first time I realized just how good men (OK, people in general) can be at lying and hiding things. It was the first time I came to the conclusion that no man is ever really just a friend. And it was the first time I saw that this person, who I thought would never, ever hurt me, and who I had often felt bad for at times when my feelings were not on the same page as his, was not who I thought he was.

Before that day, I always thought he was a great guy. What is wrong with me that I can't feel what he feels, I would ask myself. And when he ultimately told me he had gotten tired of waiting, I felt responsible for the fact that we would never work out in the long run. But in reality, we never had even the slightest chance. It was hard to look back on several years of interaction and accept that I couldn't tell the difference between the truth and all of the lies. Sigh.

Pretty soon this girl, the most current girlfriend and publisher of Mackenson's "E! True Hollywood Story" came apart at the hinges and started reaching out to me expecting us to work together in some insane pursuit to make his life miserable. The worst part was her requests were usually laced with horribly racist comments.

I'll never forget that vile. She called him and his friends a "jungle of N-words" in Spanish and said she could never take a [again insert N word here] home to her parents anyway. I had zero interest in any of her madness, and I was totally appalled. Yes, Mackenson was an ass in many ways, and he had definitely earned the anger coming toward him from several directions, but his behavior did not condone her racism—nothing does.

One thing had nothing to do with the other. But he was totally blind to it. They broke up pretty quickly after everything went down, but for a long time after, Mackenson, who didn't know the terrible things she had said about him, kept this horrible girl up on a pedestal no one could bring her down from.

Eventually, he and I made our way back to our twisted and incredibly long-winded affair. And after everything that happened, his infatuation with this girl would often manage to find its way into our sheets and our arguments. One weekend, after he had already graduated and moved back to Miami, I visited him from school.

We were lying in bed watching TV, having a lazy Sunday morning before I caught the bus back to Gainesville that afternoon. I don't remember what we were watching, but he got really excited about something and slapped my hand for me to look at the TV. Just as he did that, he yelled out her name instead of mine. It's almost as if he was simultaneously yelling it out and realizing the huge crap storm that was about to envelop him.

I think it almost hurt more that he did it while doing something simple like watching TV instead of during sex, because it felt like he was still emotionally tied to her. I was so mad and so hurt that I just asked him to take me to my bus stop right away, even though my bus wasn't set to leave for another couple of hours.

The whole ride there he kept apologizing profusely and asking me if I wanted to go grab a bite or see a movie rather than sit at the bus stop and wait. But I could hardly even look at him at that point. Reluctantly he dropped me off, and I sat on the sidewalk for what I think was two or three hours until the bus came. It was a pretty sad ride up to Gainesville that day.

It's weird; Mackenson and I had never been in an actual relationship, but at this point we had messed around with each other for five years or so, and I was definitely attached. Attached to him, attached to the ever-better sex, and attached to his adoration of me. Until this other girl came along, I had always felt like Mackeson's number one girl, like the one he would do anything for and never hurt. (Of course, this was before I knew of the girlfriend back in Haiti.) And I guess when she came into the picture, I became second-tier, and my ego just couldn't handle it. Overwhelmingly. Could. Not. Handle. It.

Eventually, Mackenson and I would reconnect once again and end up messing around for another three years or so. One evening I finally got the guts to, with pain in my heart because I didn't want to hurt his feelings, tell him all of the horrible things that girlfriend/slash "reporter" had said about him, specifically the racially motivated comments. I explained to him that I had moved past my jealousy and just hated listening to him defend someone who spoke about him that way. He was shocked and visibly hurt, but I felt he had to know and stop making a fool out of himself by defending and idolizing her. Girl, bye!

Once we got past that hurdle, it was business as usual for Mackenson and me—somewhere between friends and lovers. Once I moved back to Miami after finishing grad school (part 1), I saw him regularly. He slept over at my place and I at his. And we talked a lot about how we would always be attached to each other in some way.

He'd say that he'd bet we would both marry other people but still be pulled toward one another. I would just grin and think, "No way!" but there was no need to crush his dreams or his ego in that moment. If I did find real love, why would I ever mess it up just to sleep with this tired, gone-on-way-too-long mess we called our relationship with one another? Silly. Ass. Man. I guess part of me might have believed him a little, but I refused to accept it.

Even with everything we had been through, Mackenson and I found our way back to each other time and time again. And the sex? THE SEX! It just got better and better with every passing year. I kept waiting for it to fizzle out, but the opposite happened. There were many times I wanted to detach myself once and for all, but I couldn't find that path to freedom. Until I did. Chicago would be my way out of this never-going-anywhere but so-hard-to-shake dumbfuckery. Bless you Chi city!

Once I left Miami for the Midwest in summer 2010, I had finally found a way out. And suddenly, this person who had seemed so tightly woven into the fabric my life and my skin began to fade away, but it wasn't for lack of trying. Mackenson continued to reach out frequently, with invitations to meals that would never happen and declarations of hard-ons that he was sure would get me to drop whatever I was doing and run to him, but I had become suddenly repulsed with the whole thing. None of which was helped by him flaunting his newfound success and extravagant world travels as some kind of bargaining chip or sad attempt at resuscitating an empty lust that had become emptier still throughout the years. Maybe it's because he was always trying to fetishize me or pigeonhole me into this idea he had of who I was or who he thought I couldn't be.

During our drawn-out entanglement, any time I'd ever complain or ask Mackenson for more time, attention, or commitment, he'd tell me to be honest with myself. "You don't really want a boyfriend," he'd say. If he spent all day "on" me, asking where I was or how I was doing, I would be turned off by him, and that's what he liked about me, he'd add. I'm not a relationship girl—I'm the fantasy, he asserted. "You're the red dress in a room full of black ones." And yes, sitting here, years later, maybe there is some truth to what he was saying, but there was more to me then and there is more to me now.

To be honest, those words still haunt me today when I have my inevitable, "I'm going to die alone" or "Maybe I'm just not made for love" moments, but I didn't like him deciding who I was. Sometimes, if you're not careful, you become what people say you are, but only if you let it. And hey, maybe I had done a little deciding for myself.

Mackenson would never be who I needed him to be. He was immature and often shallow, untrustworthy and full of broken, empty promises. All those years, I think I was waiting for the fire between our bodies to sustain us, but it had become consistently clear that there was nothing more there, and that would never change. There came a point when he even stopped putting any effort into the one thing that had kept us woven for so long (the sex), and it just hardly seemed worth it anymore. I wanted to move on and stop being a slave to the novelty of time that convinced us there was any reason to continue. Thankfully, eventually, I did, and I've never looked back.

Thank you Mackenson for teaching me that sometimes people aren't who they say they are, and when someone seems too good to be true, they usually are. I'm grateful that our relationship made me more discerning when it comes to romantic partners and that it showed me that good (even great) dick does not, and will not ever, a good match or relationship make. We had a *lot* of fun together over the years—but it was just that: fun. And that's OK. I wish you the best. On to the next!

Strange Love

His name was Andrew, and this was a weird one, folks. The relationship took me completely by surprise, and sometimes I still can't wrap my head around it, but it happened, and it was intense in so many different ways.

Andrew started off as a super annoying friend of a friend, not a love interest. Well, OK: he was actually interested in me from the beginning, but I was mostly just uncomfortable. He was nice enough, but I always knew his favors came with a motive. He would hang around my dorm all the time ready to jump at the chance to feed me, drive me somewhere, or get my friends and me into clubs for free (he was a promoter—I know: douchebag central). Still, I'm not an ungrateful person, so thank you, sir! I do appreciate him taking care of me when I was a scared, lost freshman, even if his motives were not the purest.

When Andrew and I first met, I was still trying to make things work with Luca long-distance. On several occasions, Andrew even drove me to the bus stop where I would catch a ride to Miami to see him. I thought that was kind of awkward, but hey, you never turn down a free ride in college!

Once we ended up driving to Miami together for a mutual friend's mom's funeral, and he arranged for me to stay with him at his parent's house, but I asked him to drop me off at Luca's house instead (we were already broken up), meaning Andrew had to come back and pick me up for the service.

And yes, in hindsight, having him take me to Luca's house was kind of a dick move, but I had never met Andrew's parents, and I didn't feel comfortable staying with them. I also felt uncomfortable with any semblance of us being anything more than friends at that point, and I had been clear with him about this. Plus I was emotional and wanted to be with the man I still loved. Luca ended up being a huge, insensitive jerk during that trip and only making things worse, but hey, I was just following my heart.

Anyway, the timeline is hazy in my mind, but as the split between Luca and I became more and more permanent into my sophomore year, I found myself increasingly hanging out with Andrew. His persistence and admiration were growing on me, and what was once a weird combination of friendship and disgust on my end slowly began to grow into something palatable. He wanted to take care of me, and it felt nice. I could sleep over at his place and not feel like we had to do anything more than cuddle and relax. And after all the man madness I had been experiencing during that time, it was nice to feel at ease with someone.

Little by little, something was definitely happening, but I still didn't feel attracted to Andrew or like I could ever be. He was sweet and made me laugh, but he was also a little off-beat (it's hard to explain) and incredibly annoying—especially around other people, when he felt the greatest need to try too damn hard and constantly show off. Today, in my 30s, I realize his whole show stemmed from the extreme insecurity he had of not being liked much as a kid (which he often talked about), but back then it was just embarrassing and exhausting.

Eventually the whole thing wore me down, and I found myself entangled in a mind-boggling charade that left me quite literally in hives and in tears. Everything changed one night after going out dancing together, along with another friend. It had gotten later than we'd intended to be out, and his apartment was much closer to the club we were at than mine or my friend's was, so we decided it made more sense for us to just stay over and go home the next morning. Once we got to his bedroom, there was a bed and a couch, and I looked over at my friend as she gave me blaring "hell no," eyes, so I was like, OK. *I'll share the bed with him. No big deal.* Because we weren't alone, I honestly didn't think anything of it.

Today I know you can never share a bed with a straight man you're not related to and expect no one to make a move, because it will happen every single time. But back then, I never thought that far ahead. Plus we had never done anything before, nor had he ever tried—not even when we had shared a bed alone, despite his known romantic feelings for me. But maybe by this time things had built up a bit more, and he saw his chance.

So in the middle of the night, there it was. His move. And oddly enough, I was into it. Things stayed pretty PG, but I still woke up the next morning with a bare chest and my hand pressed against my forehead in disbelief. And yes, our friend was still over on that couch a few feet away the whole time. Whoops! The second she looked over and asked, "Where did your lipstick go?" I knew she knew. And you see, to my friends at the time, Andrew was more like an annoying, awkward little brother of sorts, so I knew I was going to hear about it forever. And I did!

After that night, Andrew and I began to hang out more than ever, but something even more unexpected started to happen: I started noticing that he'd suddenly avoid me when we were around his fraternity brothers (many of whom I was friends with and one with whom I had slept with for a while), as well as most other mutual friends and acquaintances, sometimes even the outside world at large. And I couldn't understand it.

Like here I am, finally giving in to this guy who had been all over me for some time now, and, suddenly, he's hiding me? He wasn't exactly the most attractive or well-liked man in the world, and he wants to hide me?! Not only was I very confused, I was even more offended. So fine. If he was going to pretend that nothing was going on between us in public, I was not going to take whatever we were doing seriously. Instead I was going to date other men and sleep with them too.

To make matters even more complicated, somewhere in-between my rage and my attraction was my bubbling disgust. It made absolutely *no* sense. There were nights that we'd lie in bed and he'd just caress the outline of my body for hours. It was so intimate and peaceful. I loved it.

Sometimes I'd want to take it further, and he'd ask why I had to make everything so sexual. That bothered me and made me feel a little slut shamed, but all right. I guess what he was really trying to say, but didn't have the tact to do in a less offensive manner, was that I should try to stay in the moment, embrace it, and enjoy it, instead of always thinking of the next step (and man, do I struggle with that in general life!). I was also his first sexual partner, and I'm sure my more experienced history made him a little insecure.

There were good nights, and there were bad ones. Like the ones when I'd wake up next to him sweating, literally breaking out in hives and struggling to breathe, with absolutely no idea why it was happening. I remember having to leave the room to regain composure and write out my feelings before I could get back into bed. He slept through the whole thing and was none the wiser the next morning when I'd be downright mean to him, and he couldn't figure out why.

As I write this all out, I realize how completely bizarre the whole relationship was, but it gets worse. In the midst of all of the rampant miscommunication and growing attraction/disgust/hiding/hives (seriously, WTF was happening?), things came to a head in an awful way.

One night Andrew showed up at my apartment unannounced while I was in my bedroom with someone else. My window was right next to the front door, so I could hear him knocking. I froze and could only think to turn off the lights like a big ol' wholly unprepared dummy. He called my cell phone, and I shut off the ringer as soon as I could, but clearly I wasn't fooling him. I don't remember if I went on with my night or asked the other guy to leave after I sensed that Andrew had walked way, but I did know that the damage was done, and I had made it exponentially worse by not facing it head on.

Although I had acted immaturely, I didn't feel like I owed him anything. We hadn't discussed being exclusive (which I wasn't even sure I wanted, per the hives and sweats), and he refused to acknowledge me in front of anyone he knew. Like the night (before the whole catching-me-with-another-guy fiasco) when I had a panic attack in a club (the worst I've ever had), and Andrew watched the whole embarrassing thing play out and still acted like he barely knew me. I was so embarrassed and depressed that I didn't shower for two days after that.

And all of it was a clear signal that things between us were never going anywhere, even if I did eventually manage to sort out my manic feelings for him. His ability to turn and ignore me during a time when I so clearly needed help was also a blatant sign to me that there was some undeniable evil lurking inside this man.

But somehow I was still hurt that the relationship was turning south. I tried going over to his apartment to talk about us and what had happened, but he wasn't caving in. He said he had gone over that night to ask me to make things official, and he was shocked at what he found instead. I laid on top of him crying, begging him to give me and us another chance as his ocean-blue eyes looked deep into mine and watered like crisp summer waves.

In the end, he didn't give in to me, and I know that was the best thing for both of us; to just be done with it and walk away from our always-problematic "relationship" or—as with most other romantic entanglements in my past—whatever else you want to call it.

I was devastated and also furious. But at the same time, I was relieved. I felt rejected by a man who had long chased *me*, and I still felt validated in the fact that his public denial of me had been the main reason for our ultimate demise. But today, with a far more mature heart and mind, I know that I too had a big role to play.

The truth is, I probably enjoyed Andrew's desire for me more than I ever liked him, and just as he was trying to hide me for whatever reason, I was, in my heart of hearts, a little more than embarrassed of him. And yes, I did have real feelings for him somewhere in the midst of all this back-and-forth tug of a mess going on inside at that time, but I obviously wasn't in any way, shape, or form ready to commit to him or anything of the sort.

I know I didn't always respond to our issues (or *my* issues) in the most mature way. But I still don't think that I should have sat around and waited for him to make up his mind or that I should have carried myself as if we were exclusive when we weren't and had never had a conversation about it.

For me, it wasn't so much that I wanted or needed him to announce to the world that we were a "thing," but the not-acknowledging-me-in-public-at-all part that really pissed me off. At the end of the day, actions really do speak volumes louder than words, and that was the ultimate insult to me. It told me that he wasn't serious about me, and more than that, he was never truly my friend. Why should I be respectful when he showed no such respect to me?

It kills me that as women we're expected to sit around perfect, pure, and true, even when the other party is not doing the same for us. Even when they're showing us zero respect, we're deemed unworthy for keeping our options open and doing what, at that point in a relationship, I believe we have every right to do (which is *not* a form of cheating).

This isn't the only time in my life I've heard some version of, "I was *going* to make it official, but *you* . . ." Yes, I'm imperfect and I mess up (quite often, in fact), but I'm not the solely responsible person in any relationship, and I'll sit around and wait for a man when he deserves it.

After Andrew and I ended things, I ran into him on campus several times a week, and sometimes I even hid behind trees to avoid him when I could manage it. Every time I saw him I was filled with rage. I often thought of taking a different route to class to avoid him, but my ego thought that would somehow make me weak or that it would mean I was letting him win.

I'll never forget I was taking a stress-management class whose professor happened to tell the class that if taking a different path to our destination meant avoiding stress, there is no shame in doing so. He even said it was the smartest thing we could do for ourselves. So I promptly took his advice and made my life a whole lot easier while I worked my way past the sordid Andrew ordeal.

He was part of my social circle, so I'd still continue to see him throughout the rest of college, but it got increasingly easier as I moved on to taller, darker, and more handsome pastures. He too moved on and ended up dating one girl for several years. I would see them out often, but it was OK. Once I got past my temporary lapse of reality, I was back to finding him incredibly annoying, overbearing, and generally unattractive.

Eventually, years after we had both graduated from college and things had ended with his long-time girlfriend, he began to reach out occasionally through social media. Once during this time we actually both hung out with a mutual friend, and Andrew was—surprise, surprise—mostly annoying, but he could definitely still make me laugh.

A few months before I found out he was suddenly (or seemingly so) engaged, we had been chatting online quite a bit, talking about planning an outing again with that same friend. Andrew even told me he thought about me a lot and would always have a special place for me in his heart.

And although I had no romantic interest in him whatsoever, enough time had passed and he seemed mature enough that I was down to hang out and be friendly. But again, probably just a few months after one of our last conversations, I found out he had gotten engaged (I didn't even know he had a girlfriend!). So there you have it. Even the dorky, annoying ones will be sneaky and try to get one over on you. And yes, it's maddening, but while it used to surprise me, now I just laugh. What else can ya do, right?

Today Andrew seems happily married, and I'm glad for him. Truly. I couldn't care less who he is or isn't with, but I also can't lie and act like he didn't play a memorable role in my journey to love or lack thereof. Like all those who came before him, he was simply not the one for me, and that's OK. In fact, it's more than OK.

Thank you Andrew for showing me that I'll always prefer to be judged for who I am than loved (or hated) for who I'm not (or pretend to be). It may sound bizarre, but I'm grateful that you hid me from others; it once again reminds me that, even when I was young and a hot mess, I still had enough self-love and self-respect fighting to live in my heart that I could recognize when I wasn't being treated the way I deserve. I'm also glad I didn't end up with someone I would undoubtedly grow to hate. Who needs that?

Nigerian Pastures

And now, ladies and gentlemen, it's time for what is probably one of my most intense memories of love and pain from my college and graduate school (round one) years, that is, my early 20s. This is the story of Tafari, a gorgeous, entrancing Nigerian man I met on the night I graduated from college. He and I would go on to be involved throughout graduate school and into early 2009, when our final, and very cruel, goodbye would transpire in the most explosive way possible.

It all began on a fateful night in May of 2006 (yes, the chronology of it all is much clearer in my head with this one!). I had just graduated with my undergraduate degree from University of Florida earlier that day, and I went out with girlfriends that evening to celebrate while my visiting family stayed back at my apartment to relax.

Funny thing is, Tafari wasn't interested in me at first. He tried to dance with my friend, who promptly rejected him. I looked up at this tall, dark, and gorgeous man thinking, "Shoot, I'll take him!" You know what they say: one woman's trash is another woman's treasure. So I immediately worked my way into his sightline and started dancing with him, completely uninvited but entirely and quickly welcomed.

Tafari towered over me like a palm tree over hot sand, and he didn't look like anyone I'd ever met before. His rich skin and chiseled, almost God-like features were only compounded by the butterflies that zipped through my stomach when I asked him his name. He reached down to whisper it in my ear with a British accent I had never heard before. I swear it was just like butter—smooth, decadent, and just the perfect spread to complete this mouth-watering snack that stood before me—eager, smiling, and ready and willing to break my heart in a whole new world-crumbling way.

I went home with him that night, because, well, that's just how it went back in those days. Actually, I went over to his place because my family was at mine, and I snuck back into my own apartment before anyone woke up the next morning (yes, at 21 and a college graduate, because that's just how you do with Cuban parents!).

That night he told me I was his first Cuban girl, which he seemed to find very exciting. I said he was my first Nigerian guy. Neither of us were surprised. We were both just completely entranced. Smiling like fools. Melting into one another like long-time lovers, not first-time strangers. And that was it. Or so I thought.

In my mind, at the end of that night, I would probably never see this magical man again, and I was OK with that. I didn't know much about him, but I assumed anything between us would never be as perfect as that night. Part of me wanted to leave it like that—untouched, untainted, and only painted with pleasure. No fuss. No reality. No pain.

We did exchange numbers, but I didn't think anything of it. And a few days later I was off to Miami for the summer before starting my graduate program, also at University of Florida, in the fall. The weeks turned into months, and although I thought about that night from time to time, I wasn't too pressed about it. It was simply a nice memory to drift into once in a while. Talk about a graduation present for the books!

I didn't realize that we would be in the same graduate program the night we met, but that's exactly what happened. I was working on my master's degree in mass communication, specializing in journalism, and he was doing the same, except he was specializing in public relations and already in his second year when I started.

We never ended up having a class together, but that journalism building/school was *small*, y'all, and it would become the battleground of our entanglement. It's actually quite interesting that I had never seen or met him before, because I also did my undergraduate degree out of that same college. I guess the universe had a specific plan for us in mind.

I first reencountered Tafari at an orientation for our graduate program during which he spoke on a panel of students to welcome the newbies and answer our questions. Watching him up on the stage, so eloquent and bright, and still gorgeous as ever, I couldn't help but fill up with rosy-colored dreams of a future together. The best part was he wasn't awkward with me *at all*. In fact, he seemed genuinely excited and perfectly comfortable to see me again, even in a setting as wildly different from the one we had originally met in.

Shortly thereafter, Tafari and I ended up seeing each other often. We'd study together. Take breaks together. Grab meals together. And, of course, sleep together. But he was always upfront with me: he had come all the way from Nigeria to pursue his graduate education and take his career to the next level, and he didn't feel like he had the time or the energy to put into an all-out relationship. I, of course, didn't listen.

Instead I continued to invest my time and my heart into him, despite what he had repeatedly told me about where he was in his life and his thought process. Pretty soon, as one might expect, I was in some deep, deep shit of my own making (and maybe a little of his too).

Every time I saw Tafari, and each time he was inside me, my feelings for him only grew stronger. In my eyes, he was amazing and unlike any man I'd ever known. He was so smart, so ambitious, so elegant, so gorgeous, so funny. And his manhood? That was unlike any I'd ever known before too, in the best way imaginable. Just thinking about it, even all these years later, is enough to send a tingling down my spine. Aye!

But pretty soon our seemingly harmless dance became toxic and unsustainable as these poorly aligned situations tend to do. I had fallen too hard, and he was committed like salt to a pretzel to his "too busy with school, no time for a relationship" spiel. He'd also tease me because I was so much younger than him—eight years to be exact. He'd tell me how at 16, he was babysitting eight year olds like me. All right. Uncomfortable comparison to make about someone you're sleeping with!

What had once been a fairly easy-breezy adventure began to stink of rejection and pain. Tafari started to reject me for other plans—which he rarely did before things got intense. He also started saying random and low-handedly cruel things like, "If you just lost a little weight, you could stop traffic," and "You really shouldn't be so honest with men about your feelings for them, because they will take advantage of you. I wouldn't do that because I'm your friend, but others might."

Oh but take advantage he did. Things were always on his schedule. He'd ignore me when he felt like it and invite me over on his whim, even if it was only to swiftly ask me to go home once he was done with my body and had to "get back to work." He was dry, insensitive, and closed off, although, to be honest, I guess he had always been that way, even when things seemed better, more hopeful, and more peaceful.

Eventually I broke down, with tears in my eyes, and begged him to open up to me a little bit. In our most intimate moments, I was sure he felt at least some of what I did, I explained to him. Sex as deep and raw (absolutely no puns intended!) as we had doesn't happen without some degree of feelings (or some degree of sociopathy on at least one side, but I knew and still know the latter was not the case with him.). And when we were good, we were *so* good. The chemistry—physical, emotional, and intellectual—was so on point that you could draw a straight line between our souls.

And, finally, for one glorious, fleeting moment, he gave me what I had been craving so badly for months: a simple but rich moment of delicious vulnerability. Tafari agreed he did in fact have feelings for me, strong feelings at that, and he said he couldn't handle watching me cry. He went on to explain that much of his seemingly insensitive or closed off demeanor was cultural.

In Nigeria, he said, you aren't taught to show your feelings, much less cry openly. So me being the complete opposite of that, super open and vulnerable, was not something he knew how to deal with. I went on to explain my side and how I'd always been this extreme "wear your feelings on your sleeve" kind of girl. Even when I wanted to hold back a little or chill out, it felt nearly impossible and fully unnatural for me to do so. I explained that I never meant to stress him out or make him feel pressured to be with me in a greater capacity then he was ready to be. I just couldn't, no matter how hard I tried, ignore what I knew was emotionally very much there.

So OK. Fair. I appreciated him taking the time to tell me more about why he acted the way he did and how he felt. It was also nice to get the opportunity to help him understand me a little better too. The conversation didn't necessarily change or fix anything, but it helped us have a better understanding of one another. Eventually, though, we would still crumble. I wanted—no, I *needed*—more, and he was fiercely unwilling to give it to me. So for the couple of months before he graduated that year and left Gainesville, we'd only see each other during forced run-ins at school.

Initially, it didn't take long at all for me to feel OK. Sure I missed him, but our split had not been anything super explosive, mostly just a case of misaligned interests. Of course, it was never fun running into him at school, especially once I began to suspect he was seeing one of the other girls in our program, but I had definitely been in much bigger states of heartbreak before. I also knew he would graduate soon and my time having to deal with his presence was limited.

It wouldn't be until our second ring around the rosy that my world would be turned upside down and I'd spiral into what is still one of the worst bouts of depression I've ever experienced.

It was late 2008, and Tafari's birthday was coming up. I'm not the best with birthdays, but I knew it was sometime around Thanksgiving. At this point it had probably been a year and a half, give or take, since we had last seen or spoken to each other. By that time, I had graduated too and was back in Miami working as a marketing project manager for a nonprofit.

I don't know what came over me, but I suddenly decided it was a good idea to reach out and wish him a happy birthday. I sent him a happy birthday greeting in the form of a Facebook message, you know, trying to be super nonchalant about it. To my surprise, he responded almost immediately and told me it was so good to hear from me. He said his dad was in town (Tafari had ended up in Houston after graduation) visiting him from Nigeria, and they had just gone Black Friday shopping. How cute, I thought.

That night, Tafari and I had quite the chat. He said he had messed up so badly letting me go before and that he never wanted to lose me again. GASP. I was, as you can imagine, both shocked and beside myself to hear these words come from the last person on earth I ever expected them to come from.

We continued chatting over the next few days and weeks, and pretty soon he had booked a ticket to come see me in Miami. Going to pick him up at the airport (this was pre-rideshares!), I felt so excited and nervous all at once that I stood somewhere in-between smiles, tears, and all-out throw up. I had no idea what would come of the weekend, and I certainly hadn't expected the sweet turn of events before me.

Tafari walked out of the airport just as I pulled up. Forget ear to ear; I'm pretty sure the man was grinning from ear to navel. He ran to me sort of like they do in those sappy, romantic movies when long-lost lovers run across the beach to catch one another. We embraced for what felt like the greatest hug that had ever ensued between two bodies. And off we went into the night.

We spent that weekend fucking (duh), shopping, and visiting my parents. The first night in-between tongue waltzes and soft moans (even while we were still standing up), he whispered in my ear that I'd always been such an amazing kisser and nothing had changed (it still hasn't, wink, wink!). I died a little inside in the best kind of way.

The next couple days were easy, romantic, and absolutely heavenly. We sat up in bed talking like I don't think we'd ever done before. We might have even forgotten a condom a couple of times as he declared he'd be totally fine if I got pregnant. I was 23 and didn't know what the hell I wanted, but I knew I liked this new, committed Tafari and the starkly different kind of attention he was suddenly giving me. Today I know I was being a gigantic dumbass, but hindsight is always 20/20, isn't it? Luckily, I didn't get pregnant or contract a disease, so thank my lucky stars for that one. Phew!

During our bedtime chats, Tafari and I discussed finishing graduate school, working, money, and all that good stuff. I had a master's degree, but I was only in my early 20s and no one cared (and I mean no one!), so I was making little money and barely making it, even living with a roommate. To make a point, I said something about how hard I had to think just to buy something as simple and relatively inexpensive as work shoes (you know, back in the day when having closed-toed shoes for work was a must for women).

I genuinely wasn't asking for anything (it's never been my style to rely on anyone for financial help), but he instantly offered to take me shopping. He couldn't have me stressing out about work shoes, he insisted. So with me feeling super awkward and embarrassed, and him feeling happy to be able to do this for me, we headed to the mall.

I think we went to Macy's, where he ended up buying me the two most expensive pairs of shoes I had ever owned, along with a few other things. The whole experience was bizarre. I don't think I'd ever been on such a shopping trip with a man before. And, sure, we were there together and having our little weekend of playing house, but we weren't actually *together* together, so when the sales lady started asking questions about our relationship (nosy much?), I let him take the lead.

Later that weekend we went to see my parents, and I never, ever take men home to my parents. In fact, the last time I had taken a man to meet them before that was when I had boyfriends (Diego and Luca) in high school and had no choice in the matter. Because most of my relationships until that point had been situationships through and through, I didn't see the point in involving them. That and I didn't want questions and over-involvement of any sort. Dating is already hard enough as it is, am I right?

The only reason I even took Tafari there, after much convincing (he was dying of embarrassment/shyness) was because after learning that he was African, my dad was more excited than a little kid eating cookies before dinner. You see, my dad's great grandmother was

African, and he even speaks the same African language that Tafari speaks because of his (my dad's) religion, an Afro-Cuban form of Santeria.

I felt awkward about the whole thing, but I didn't want to disappoint my dad. He was so damn excited. Tafari was nervous and hesitant, but he agreed to go. So we went, and within minutes my dad had busted out the photo album, you know, the *really* old kind with photos crumbling at the edges and yellow from the wear and tear of time.

There she was—my African great, great grandmother in all her glory. Tafari couldn't believe his eyes. I'm not sure why he'd think I'd make something like that up, but it was obvious he hadn't been convinced of her validity until he stood face to face with her picture and my dad's stories.

Tafari glanced back and forth between the album and me with a twinkle in his eye and a grin on his cheeks like he had fallen in love with me in that moment. It was as if he was seeing the deep connection to his roots in the kink of my hair and the melanin of my skin for the very first time.

Before I knew it, our enchanted weekend was over, and it couldn't have gone any better. He was sticking around for one more night but went to spend it with another friend (a guy, or I would have surely lost my shit!) he knew in town who he hadn't seen in a while. If I close my eyes right now, I can see him standing on the other side of the doorstep smiling as tears filled my eyes.

"It's OK," he reassured me. "We're always just phone call or a plane ride away," he whispered.

"And what if I leave Miami?" I asked. (I had been dreaming and scheming of moving to Chicago).

"Then I'll come to Chicago," he said.

And with that, sadness transformed into hope.

In the weeks after his visit, I ended up moving to an efficiency apartment on my own, and things were crazy. We continued to talk all the time, and he wanted to see me again—fast. I wanted to see him too, but I didn't have the time or money for a flight to Houston. I'd also traveled infrequently back then, so the whole thing was far more intimidating than it would be today.

We began exchanging heated (sexually) texts as we both sat at work trying to maintain our composure. Once we both excused ourselves to our respective office bathrooms and proceeded to have what I didn't even know was a thing at the time—full-blown text sex! It was quick, but it was wild. I would have surely died had anyone heard or seen anything, but alas, they didn't, and here I am today telling the world anyway. What a time to be alive!

Pretty soon Tafari was telling me he couldn't take it any longer. He *had* to see me. "Find a flight and tell me how much it is. I'll send you the money," he said. So I did. Despite a brand new move and the worst possible timing for me, I packed a duffel bag (I didn't even have proper luggage!) and headed to Houston for what was destined to be one of the worst weekends of my life. But I didn't know that as I packed my bag full of excitement and hope for the future, and for much of our first night together, I still wouldn't.

From the minute I arrived in Houston, everything that could go wrong did. The airline lost my bag, so I was left with nothing but my purse and the clothes on my back. When the attendant at the airport told me my bag hadn't made it, it was my worst nightmare realized. I called Tafari to let him know the situation, and he assured me that we'd make it work, which immediately comforted me, but I still felt so naked without my things.

He picked me up, and we headed off to dinner at The Melting Pot. On the way to the restaurant, I called my parents to check in, and my dad asked to speak to Tafari, who told my dad not to worry and that he'd take good care of me. Later, still on the same drive to the restaurant, Tafari picked up a call from a friend. He told him he was with "Sonia." I assume the guy asked who that was, because Tafari replied, very matter of factly, "My girlfriend." Um OK! No one had told me about all of this sudden officiality, but I was definitely into it. Despite the luggage fiasco, I was starting to feel like a very lucky lady.

We finally arrived at the restaurant and proceeded to have the most romantic dinner I'd ever shared with a man. We sat close, we talked and laughed, and we even fed each other food. It was the most relationship-y night I had experienced in a really long time, and the first time I'd ever seen Tafari in such rare, magnificent form.

After dinner we went to Walmart, where Tafari bought me a toothbrush and a pair of underwear to make it until my bag was found and delivered, which was supposed to happen sometime the next day. It all felt thoughtful and sweet, and it definitely helped me feel better about having almost nothing with me and being completely out of my comfort zone.

It wasn't until we got back to his apartment and I took a shower that everything started to fall apart, never to come back together again. I slipped in his shower and fell super hard to the floor, leaving me with a pounding headache and an aching back. It also just scared the shit out of me. There was no blood, but I felt totally off after the fall. And it only served to compound the already-present stress of my missing bag. Tafari gave me some over the counter painkillers, and that was pretty much the end of his concern or sensitivity with the situation.

All I really wanted to do at that point was crawl into bed and go to sleep, but he had other ideas. No more than probably five or 10 minutes after he slapped his pill Band-Aid on me and sent me on my way to everything-is-suddenly-OK-ville, he was ready to fuck. Me being a young people pleaser (specifically to men) of the worst kind, I didn't assert my desire, or lack thereof, to stop. So we had the sex (which I still somehow managed to enjoy), my body continued to ache, and eventually we went to sleep—finally!

The next morning I still felt a little off from the fall and secretly annoyed at Tafari for his tepid sensitivity. But as I tend to do, I tried to be positive and shake it off. He went to work, and I had all day to relax. Pretty soon I was bored out of my mind. He had made absolutely no arrangements for me to do anything while he was gone, and I was pretty much stuck in this apartment in completely unknown territory, still without my things. Today I would have ventured out on my own just fine, but back then, having traveled so little before and being so broke, my options were extremely limited.

I'm not even sure he had much to eat in the place, but I made the best of it and decided to clean the apartment for him as a nice gesture. Thankfully, at some point that day, my bag was delivered to the apartment, and I could at least feel like a person again. But I was still so *bored*. Not only had Tafari not bothered to take the day off (like I had to do to be there with him at his insistence) but he also didn't even come home right after work. Instead he went to some kind of after-hours doctor's appointment and didn't get home until almost 8:00 p.m. To add insult to injury, he wasn't thrilled that I had cleaned up his place either. He didn't like that I had been all up in his things. Excuse the hell out of me for trying to do something nice and not lose my mind in the process of waiting for you to get home, sir.

Still I stayed upbeat and positive, and eagerly asked what we were doing that night. He still had NOTHING to offer me. I think we ended up ordering dinner in, but what I do vividly remember is the after-dinner part of the evening. We sat around sipping wine and listening to music. Which OK, it was nice, but I would have still liked to go out after being stuck in the apartment all day alone.

Being the cheap date that I *still* am, it didn't take much wine at all before I was feeling a little intoxicated and very free with the heart and the tongue. We were sitting on the couch, me bitching (in the nicest way possible) about his lack of planning and making zero effort to properly host me, and him offering me his lame excuses while smiling at me like my grievances were almost cute or funny to him—cheeky even, as he would often say.

And then I did it. Despite having been fairly annoyed with him for most of the day, I suddenly felt an uprising in my chest that caused me to tell Tafari that I loved him in a wine-induced slip of the over-emotional and over-eager tongue. That was the blinding moment the trip really came crashing down all around me with no hope of any survivors.

His response to my "I love you," was something to the tune of, "Thank you. I'm not there yet, but it doesn't mean I won't get there." OK fine. No biggie, right? But then he continued: "Besides, I can't really get serious with you right now, because I already have a girlfriend." It felt like a bomb had just gone off in my ears. Come again?

What in the hell am I doing sitting on this couch with you in Houston, Texas, by way of a plane ticket YOU bought me and on a trip YOU insisted I take, because YOU allegedly simply *could not* bear to go any longer without seeing me again? And hadn't he just called *me* his girlfriend the night before? This was the combination of thoughts in my head and actual words I spewed back as the shrapnel from his sudden declaration struck me over and over again.

It turns out this girlfriend of his was back home in Nigeria and had been in his life on and off for a long time, always unbeknownst to me. He pleaded with me not to be angry with him, as if the news he had just delivered was the most normal thing in the world. I couldn't even look at him. So I let him know as much and asked that we please go to bed.

I'm not sure how I slept that night, but I know it took at least an hour for my legs to stop shaking and the red-hot fumes coming out of my ears to settle. I woke up the next morning still angry, confused, and stunned. But where could I go? Again, I had very little money *and* very little experience traveling, so I thought OK, I just need to get through the next few days before my flight back home. I can do this. But try as I might, a nightmare still unfolded.

Over the next few days, I tried to stay positive and make the best of the situation. We went out dancing, had a few meals, went furniture shopping, caught a movie, and hung out at his apartment complex's pool. It was all so bizarre, and we began to argue at almost every turn, mostly because I didn't have it in me to act like nothing had happened and nothing had been said; like everything was A-OK, because it wasn't. How could it be?

One night we went to see whichever Madea movie (you know, those Tyler Perry joints) was out at the time, and Tafari randomly started talking about how he's not like black American people (referring to a majority of the other moviegoers) and hates when others assume he is the same. "I am African. I am not like these [N word]s." I swear I almost fell out of my chair to the ground.

He was being *so* arrogant, so disgusting, and so vile. I again struggled to look at him. I mean, I guess he is perfectly entitled to his opinions, but he was going off on these people who were not even doing or saying anything. They were simply existing. And all this from a man who constantly talked to me about how much harder he had to work to succeed as a black man in America, constantly discussing and complaining about the racism he often faced. Yet there he was—spewing the same hate he loathed so much at others.

At dinner that same night I was filled with rage and disgust from his earlier comments, which had only compounded the sheer madness of everything else that had already transpired. I continued to struggle to look at him. I was quiet and aloof, and mostly just sitting there, trying to survive. Eventually he asked me what was wrong. "What's wrong?!" I thought. Is this man for real right now?

I told him everything that was bothering me; primarily his whole, "Oh oops, by the way, I have a girlfriend," thing that he seemed to think was no big deal. He looked at me square in the eyes and said, "I'm not a monster, you know." I thought, "Oh but you are."

The next day, still trapped and miserable, I agreed to go furniture shopping with Tafari. He walked around the store, holding my hand and asking me what I thought in front of the sales guy in a way that made it sound as though we were buying furniture for a home we shared together. It was, in a word, ridiculous. Like who was this guy, what was I doing in this horrible *Twilight Zone* episode, and when would my torture end? I walked around the store with my eyes wide open in absolute disbelief, once again, just trying to survive it all.

Somewhere in-between all of these varying levels of madness, we had sex again after having enough drinks to calm my rage. But it wasn't like any time before. It was angry, detached, and even painful. Tafari had a habit of spanking me during sex (which normally was not a problem—sign me up!), but this time he did it so repeatedly and with such force that he left big purple bruises in the shape of his hands on my body. And sure, I came like I've rarely done in the many years since, but once it was all over, I felt deflated and was left squirming from the pain.

On my last night in Houston, and after a lot of bickering, I ended up sleeping on the couch. The next morning, before he came out of the bedroom, he was in the shower singing like he was just *so* happy and hadn't a care in the world. But when he came out of the bedroom, he looked at me with a particular and disturbing mix of hate and disgust that I had never seen on his, or anyone's, eyes before.

Then he asked, "What the fuck do you want for breakfast?"

"Do you really need to speak to me that way?" I asked.

I ended up choking down a bowl of tear-soaked cereal.

He was at the dining room table working on his computer when I went over and asked if we could talk. I tried to get him to understand where I was coming from and have a calm, adult discussion, but he wasn't interested. Instead he called my airline to see if he could get me an earlier flight back to Miami, but it was astronomically expensive. He knew I certainly couldn't afford any of the fees, and at that point he was obviously not interested in paying my way either.

Still set on getting rid of me as quickly as possible, Tafari dropped me off at the airport four hours before my flight. In the car he blasted music (that Pussycat Dolls song, "I Hate This Part," was playing on the radio, which was eerily and gut-wrenchingly on point at that moment), sang loudly, and banged his hands on the gearstick as if to signify his soul dancing. All of this as I sat next to him crumbling.

"You don't have to act so fucking happy, you know," I insisted. He smirked and side-eyed me, said nothing in response, and carried on with his cruel joy concert. And after what seemed like an eternity burning in hell, we arrived at the airport.

He got out of the car to get my bag from the trunk, but he refused to look at me or say anything. I hugged his waist (imagine all 5'3 of me grabbing all 6' plus of him) and pleaded with him not to let things end this way as tears of pain and confusion choked through my words. But he never budged, and so eventually I let go. He got in the car and peeled off, and I walked into the airport with my soul in my hands.

Everyone looked at me with sympathy and questions in their eyes; they were probably wondering what could have possibly happened to this young woman to make her look like such a wreck. I was embarrassed but unable to hide my raw emotional dismemberment. Once I finally got to my gate, I sat in the waiting area and cried for hours. Then I cried the whole flight home, as well as in the car with my dad, who came to pick me up. I tried to tell him a little bit of what happened without going into too much parent-inappropriate detail, but he didn't even know what to say except, "Forget him!" If only it had been that easy. It would end up being at least a year before airports stopped making me soul-suckingly sad.

I spent the next couple days texting Tafari, begging him for answers. This isn't about fixing things between us or anything like that, I tried to explain. I just needed answers. I needed to know why. But he never replied and promptly blocked me on social media. I never heard from him again, and that bitter goodbye at George Bush

Intercontinental Airport would be the last time I ever laid eyes on that cruel, beautiful man.

A few years ago, a friend of mine somehow happened to come across Tafari on Facebook and saw that he had married a Mexican woman, despite his prior insistence that he would need to eventually marry someone from Nigeria, like him. But hey, God bless. I know now that he was not the one for me (despite the fact that I definitely had wedding altar dreams about him on several occasions!). I hope he's the best version of himself for her and that he's happy. And if I ever happen to cross his mind, I hope that he remembers me as a good woman who never wanted anything more than to love him.

Thank you Tafari for teaching me that dreams, like this very book, don't have expiration dates (he always used to say that, and it has really stuck with me). I'm grateful for all of the beautiful stories you told me about Africa and how you opened up my world at a time when I had seen very little of it. Thank you for helping me feel less alone in the study struggle during my first year of grad school, when I was only 21 and feeling incredibly overwhelmed and out of place. Thank you for inspiring me to keep pushing through it all.

Thank you for being the first person to teach me that just because a man is good on paper (educated, ambitious, funny, adventurous, and successful) doesn't mean he won't break your heart into a million pieces or have an ugly side. Thank you for teaching me that no matter how small someone else makes me feel, I will always find a way to pick myself up from under their shoe and find my light again.

And finally, thank you for spiraling me into the deep depression that pushed me to finally make the move to Chicago, where I had dreamed of living since I first visited it in 2007. After you left me so broken, I felt like I could barely breathe until I made a drastic change in my life.

Thank you!

Disaster Days

The relationships in this chapter are just some of the highlights, if you can call them that, of my college romances. Any time in-between was pretty much spent looking for love in *all* of the places; places whose names I mostly don't remember. I spent my time seeking attention and validation in arms that only wanted to play, not hold. It was a wild, sometimes tragic, ride, but it was mostly a ton of fun and a big learning experience for me. I came out of those years more self-aware, confident, and hopeful than ever, and for that I am truly grateful.

CHAPTER 4
Miami Dater's Nightmare, Part 1:
Connection Stagnation

Bodies are easy to connect in lust, but great minds require a little more magic to find each other.

Before and after Tafari seeped into my Miami existence, and somewhere in-between my tired rendezvous with Mackenson, my first time dating (also known as trying to find Mr. Right) in Miami as an adult after graduate school was filled with misfires and misfits; lots of guys who were mostly sweet but not very smart. It was fun, but more often than not, it was suffocating.

A Fall from Grace

First there was Nathan, whom I met at work and was inexplicably drawn to despite his bad-boy reputation and general lack of direction in life. He was so sexy that I even found myself running to the complete opposite side of the office, through a long hallway and too many people to hide from, just to flirt with him at his desk. And in those days, that was a big deal for me. I was at my first full-time job out of school, where my goody two-shoes naiveté and a fairly strict-for-no-good-reason work environment usually had me scared into silence and submission.

For the better part of a year, Nathan swore up and down the street and around the corner that he didn't like me "like that," but his fiery flirtation told me otherwise. But OK, fine. I eventually resigned myself to being friends (although I use that word as lightly as I'd throw a feather), which was still fun because every interaction between us seemed laced with flirty laughter and suggestive innuendo. And when it wasn't fun, it was pure torture, because I had to see him every day at work.

Then there were all the times that we made plans to hang out outside of work, and he'd stand me up at the last minute time and time again—and there I'd be, all dressed up with my heart in my hand and nowhere to go but all night to think.

I cried in the car on the way to work more than once, especially when certain songs like Leona Lewis's "Bleeding Love" came on the radio—remember that jam? And let's be clear: when I say crying, what I really mean is balling like a soiled baby. "How could this be happening to me *again*?" I wondered. Another man who says I'm amazing and spends his time flirting and laughing with me, seeking me out, and making plans with me, but when it really counts, he's never there; he always lets me down.

Eventually, after everything he put me through (and I put myself through for sticking around for the abuse), Nathan confessed that he did in fact have feelings for me and always had. The night it all came to a head, we were in my car talking as I tried to figure out how this whole thing could possibly be one-sided when the tension in the air was so thick that you could practically scoop it up with your hand and take a bite out of it.

The kiss that followed that conversation was our first, and it was intense. Before it happened, his leg shook and my heart exploded as we looked at each other in a desperate duel to figure out who was going to break the tension and make the first move. I certainly wasn't going to give in after all the times he had rejected me, even if I did feel the inevitability of the impending explosion of passion brewing in that little car.

Eventually, we cornily and cutely agreed that we were going to go for it and give in to everything that had been boiling up between us for months. And it was just . . . WOW. I could barely believe it as it was happening, but its magic didn't make things any simpler.

After that night we tried to make something out of our encounter and slept together a few times (it was far more anticlimactic than the kiss, I'll tell ya), but eventually he went back to standing me up, running away from his feelings, and breaking my heart for sport, and the whole thing dissolved into another painful memory to add to my ever-growing list.

Through the years, Nathan and I stayed connected on social media and occasionally had random conversations through Facebook Messenger, but by that point, I had moved on from what was obviously much more a grand fantasy in my head than anything else. Still, as my pattern dictates, I ended up hanging out with him when I was living away from Miami but in town for a few days. I was bored at my parents' house, and he had learned I was in town from my social media updates. He reached out and asked if I was around and wanted to get a drink. What the hell else was I doing, right? I said, "Sure!"

So we had the drinks. Pretty soon we were laughing and giggling, and he told me that he had always liked me back in the day, even when he acted like he didn't. In fact, he told me he was actually in love with me then, but he had been too busy trying to be Rico Suave, which roughly equates to a "mack daddy" of sorts, and unprepared to settle down.

I couldn't believe my ears for several reasons, one of which was having spent all that time being stood up by him and getting my heart broken left and right, believing he wasn't into me and thinking maybe I wasn't good enough for him. And all because he wasn't ready or was unable to deal with his feelings for me? How rude! Second, it's damn near the story of my life—this "I loved you, but I was too scared" game. And third, I couldn't believe I was being validated to such an extent after having gone out that night for no other reason than I had nothing else to do and figured it might be fun to hang out.

Inevitably, as the drinks kept flowing along with his compliments, I had the grand idea and suggestion that we hook up. He was like, "Yeah!" But I was just visiting, and therefore staying with family, and he—being the hot mess he always was—had been crashing on someone's couch. So we decided to go to a motel. Minus the laughable stripper pole and lip-shaped sofa in the room, we had a great time that night.

When we got there I was so nervous I almost felt like a teenager again. It had been about six months since I had been with anyone, plus it was *Nathan*. Now that he had confessed his true and long-held feelings for me, everything had changed and multiplied. It had almost become more electrifying, even though he was no longer quite the looker he had been eight years before (although who is, right?).

After that night, I went back to New York City, where I was living, and wouldn't see Nathan again for a while—until I moved back to Miami in fall 2016.

I had a traumatic time my second and last year in New York plagued by loneliness, the worst and most aggressive sexual harassment I had ever experienced, and the most intense physical fear I had ever felt (that's a story for a whole other book!). So when I decided to come back home, I needed a lot of comfort; I needed to feel safe and loved. For both that reason and financial ones, I bunked with family my first year back in Miami. I also initially sought comfort in the arms that were most readily available to me at the time—Nathan's.

Most of my issues with New York stemmed from my interactions with men, and, as a result, I had closed myself off to dating. I was also going through a terrible bout of depression and desperately trying to figure out my next move, so there wasn't any room in my spirit to do much more than get my work done, constantly eat my feelings, and survive—or at least try to.

As soon as I got back to Miami and started to feel safer and happier (almost immediately!), I also began to feel a little out of sorts staying with family. The whole zero privacy thing after being on my own and away from home for such a long time, almost consistently since I was 17, was hard. Going over to Nathan's was a way to sort of feel like an adult, even though it meant hanging out in a practically empty house with all of one fork and one spoon and sleeping on an air mattress.

The bathroom was also a little suspect, and my New York–induced fear of mice was definitely on my mind when I was at his place. Still, for a few weeks, we had fun in this less than desirable setup. We cuddled, ordered food, watched TV, messed around, and slept. It was easy, warm, and comforting.

But soon the condition of his place started to creep me out too much, and we got into a political argument (this was fall 2016 after all, an election year!). And even though we ended said argument by agreeing to disagree, after that night I felt him start to distance himself and avoid me. I fought it for a week or two, but soon I let go.

I reminded myself that it was my ego that was offended and not my heart that was broken. And that I should be honest with myself about the reality of the situation, no matter how much I craved the attention. Because let's be real: I wasn't serious about him, and he had nothing to offer me in the long-term. Sometimes I think it wasn't the political argument that made things weird but maybe his realization that I was using him. I sincerely didn't mean to, but quickly realized I was doing just that. And although he had used and mistreated me in the past, maybe he really did have feelings for me now and saw that the tables had turned.

It's funny how something that once felt so unattainable and I was so heartbroken by could suddenly lose its luster to such a degree. That's the thing about growing up; you become more honest with yourself about who you are, who other people are, and what you do and don't deserve. And one day it becomes exponentially easier to move on.

Thank you Nathan for making me laugh until I cried many times over. I am grateful that the pain I once felt for you over your antics turned into a realization that I was always worth much more than you could ever offer me. I hope I never hurt you the way you once hurt me. And if I did, I hope you know I didn't mean to. I guess sometimes you just become what you've been given.

Sweet Nothing

And now for a much lighter tale, let's move on to one of my fonder memories of dating in Miami, even if it did still eventually end up in mild flames a couple years later. I'm talking about Bobby, an adorable guy who was 21 when I met him at 24. And at the time those three years between us felt like an eternity of difference.

I remember it like it was yesterday: I was at a nightclub with friends late one night, when I looked over and noticed a guy summoning someone with his finger in a come-hither fashion. I looked behind me, trying to figure out who he was talking to, but saw no one. Then I realized he was actually looking at me. I usually wouldn't respond to this kind of foolishness, but he was really cute, and I would be lying if I said I wasn't flattered. I also preferred a come-hither finger summoning over a grind-up-behind-me-without-permission move any day.

So I walked over and started talking to him as we danced. He immediately made me laugh and feel at ease. We danced for a while, until my friends let me know they were leaving. We exchanged numbers, and a few days later we were off to Dave & Buster's on our first date. We shared drinks, games, and more laughs. He even won me a super cute teddy bear that we named after him, and I still have in a memory box somewhere!

Perhaps sadly, I was pretty impressed by his approach of taking me on a date instead of just asking to come over to my place like most guys did. We ended the night with him walking me to my car and kissing me goodnight in a delicious hot-sweet kind of way. Cute, right?

Our beginning had all of the makings of a great relationship, but as with 98 percent of the romantic encounters in my life, it didn't turn into anything serious—just another situationship, although one that didn't break me and was generally and consistently enjoyable.

Bobby was never the brightest crayon in the box, but he was sweet; unpretentious; funny; fun; loving; and, dare I say, almost magical in bed. The first time we slept together (after a month of dating—I was trying something new!), he stopped us in the middle of it and actually asked me if I wanted an Oscar for my performance. Excuse me?

I'm naturally enthusiastic in bed, but he took that to mean I was putting on a show. "I don't know what kind of girls you've been with in the past, but there is no show," I said. "Maybe you should not fuck me so good, and then I might be quieter." At that moment I knew he had never been with a girl like me before, but he was intrigued. We carried on, despite his shock and me now feeling self-conscious about any and every noise or move I made. Eventually we figured it out though, and it was great—every single time.

Over the next year, Bobby and I hung out frequently. Sometimes we'd grab a bite to eat or a drink, and other times we'd just watch a movie in bed before having sex and falling asleep wrapped up in each other like longtime lovers. It was easy; probably one of the easiest romantic entanglements I've ever had.

But I did develop deeper feelings for him, because *of course*, and one night over dinner at a bar I asked him why we weren't boyfriend and girlfriend. My argument was simple: we had a great time together, we both seemed to be really into each other, and we were already spending a ton of time together. So what was the issue? What he said next felt genuine, although slightly unfair and unlike anything I had ever heard before during many similar conversations in the past.

Bobby looked at me with sadness in his eyes. I believe he didn't want to hurt me but knew he was about to. He said he *did* like me, but he wasn't good enough for me. He then explained that he often didn't understand anything I said when I spoke, which I found surprising, because although I'm well-educated, I never thought of myself as a formal person in any way, especially in social settings. But OK.

I guess I was torn between feeling confused and a little flattered. But more than that, I was frustrated as hell. Why couldn't he let me decide who was and wasn't good enough for me? I wanted to believe him, but a part of me couldn't help but wonder if this was just a very sensitively put copout.

I got over it, though, probably because I did end up believing he was telling me how he felt—he was a sweet guy. And regardless, it was around that time that I began to get serious about leaving Miami and moving to Chicago, so in the end, I had much bigger fish to fry.

Bobby and I continued to hang out right up until I moved to Chicago in summer 2010, and it continued to be fun, easy, and satisfying, despite him somewhat rejecting me that night at the bar. Ours wasn't a love of fairytales, but there was definitely a connection between us. And while we weren't *in* love, we did love and care for each other. For the first, and probably last, time in my life, that was enough.

For one last hurrah, Bobby came over to hang out two weeks before I left for Chicago. It was obvious from the extra-sparkly twinkle in his eyes that he had a couple of drinks before he arrived and had gotten all up in his feelings on the ride over.

For all intents and purposes, Bobby and I were little more than fuck buddies, but that had never stopped him from showing up when he said he would, being sweet and open, cuddling, and being in the moment with me rather than stipulating labels for our interactions. I really loved that about him.

Our last night together, he was extra wonderful. He told me how much he would miss me. I'll never forget how he looked into my expectant eyes and said, in that sexy *Cubanaso* (or very Cuban) voice of his, "Sonia, *yo te quiero mucho. ¿Tu me quieres a mi?*" which translates to, "Sonia, I love you very much. Do you love me?" I about melted into a puddle right down to the grooves of the tile floor beneath us. After I managed the words, "I love you too, Bobby," with a sigh of emotion, we kissed in a way that felt different from all of the other times.

Then he suggested we take our emotions into the shower, and we did—to the shower floor, specifically. I swear it was like something straight out of a *novela*. The water beat down on us like caramel pouring onto a sundae as we shared what would probably be our most intimate moments ever. It. Was. Perfect. Actually, it was more than perfect. It was sublime.

Two quick weeks later, I was off to Chicago, and that was that. I reunited with Bobby a handful of times over the next few years, although eventually it turned into little more than random "I miss you" and "Remember that time . . ." texts.

We made plans a few times that never happened, and he started to act strange, so I suspected he had a girlfriend he didn't want to tell me about, and I backed off. The last time we texted was actually not too long ago. He wanted me to help him with a paper, but after our conversation got political and a little tense, I never heard from him again, which is totally fine.

I'd rather remember Bobby as that sweet, simple guy who always made me laugh and feel good. The one who showed me emotion and respect, and never made me feel like less than just because we weren't officially together. I didn't want to think of him as a liar, a cheater, or a Republican. Sure the memory is a little tainted after his fall from the pedestal I had let his sweetness and aptitude in the boudoir put him up on, but it is still mostly positive.

In the end, Bobby is a good reminder that sometimes two people who aren't meant for each other can still share something special and that every situationship doesn't have to be heavy or negative. He's also a good reminder that love forms and exists in many different ways, and that's not less special just because it's not textbook love. Finally, he's a good reminder that often, beneath a sweet exterior, is just another asshole waiting for his moment to shine. Thank you Bobby!

Cuban Pete

Somewhere in-between Nathan and Bobby there was Manny, the almost-twice-my-age divorced coworker who I rendezvoused with on Friday nights at margarita and salsa dancing–laced happy hours that always felt like a delicious celebration of life. I had never been attracted to or even dreamed of being attracted to a man that much my senior, but Manny never felt old to me—head full of soft, curly salt and pepper hair and all. When we danced the night away, he didn't feel old. When his hands lay firmly yet softly on my hips, he didn't feel old. And when we kissed like love-hungry teenagers for what felt like hours on end, he certainly didn't feel old.

But that's all Manny and I ever did. He refused to sleep with me, because he said there had to be boundaries, and no matter how much I practically begged, he never gave in. Maybe it was the age thing or maybe it was the coworker thing, but in the end, I respect him for keeping it light. It's probably the reason I can still think of him and those times fondly. We kept in touch here and there after I left Miami in 2010, but I've never seen him again.

Manny did recently reach out asking to grab drinks and catch up, which I was totally up for and even really excited about. We made a plan two weeks in advance, and when the day came, he basically stood me up. A short time after, he called me, acting very erratically, making little sense, and randomly boasting about not needing anyone in life and not being able to meet up that night after all. Um OK! I tried to give it another chance and agreed to meet up for drinks the next day, but when the next day came, I honestly didn't feel like dealing with it or going out of my way to meet him when he had basically split on our plans the night before for no apparent reason.

It turns out I have grown too old and maybe too wise to put up with the bullshit. It's OK though. Much like Bobby, I'd rather leave Manny in the past and remember him as the fun, sweet party guy who always made me feel on top of the world when he took my hand for hours of sweet, passionate adventure on the dance floor. Because as it turns out, what's really under that "happy" party-party, fun-fun exterior is an immature pretty boy who has no intentions of growing up—not at 45, not at 50, not ever—and God bless, brother, you do you. But no thank you!

Thanks for the good times though. They were truly exceptional.

Sex Haze, Brain Daze

Then there was Luis. Three weeks of forget-your-name-and-your-to-do-list sex with Luis. We met at a bar and started hanging out almost immediately. But all we did was have sex, eat, sleep, and repeat. We did manage to get to work in-between, but it all still felt like too much, too soon. After three weeks of this, I snapped out of my sex haze and realized I had momentarily forgotten to be a person. I needed to clean, do laundry, and buy groceries, I thought. I should be seeing friends, running errands, and living my life outside of this bedroom.

As soon as I decided to tone things down and get back to myself, Luis ended up in the hospital needing gallbladder surgery. We were eating dinner at my apartment when he came down with what he thought was a bad stomachache. He immediately stopped eating and went home to rest it off. Next thing I know, he sends me a text saying he's in the hospital and needs surgery to remove his gallbladder. So, of course, even though I was starting to feel the need to pull back from our little overzealous rendezvous, I went to see him at the hospital, because it was the right thing to do.

His whole family was there, including his mother, young daughter, and ex-girlfriend/baby momma. Naturally this suddenly made our entanglement way too real and heavier than it ever needed to be, and although I played along for a little bit, I started to feel trapped and uncomfortable with the whole thing. I had only known this guy for three or four weeks, and as soon as we had crawled out from under the covers long enough to actually talk to each other, it became quickly and painfully clear that we had nothing in common. Much like Bobby, he wasn't the brightest crayon in the box—except he wasn't even the fifth brightest. I don't say that to be mean. I only say it because it made us completely incompatible.

When I tried to let Luis down easy and tell him I didn't think we had anything in common, he didn't get it, but I stayed strong. Eventually he accepted our fate and let it go. He did reach out on social media not too long ago (an attempt to connect that I promptly ignored), because as you all might have realized by now, when it comes to my life, they *always* come back. Many times even 10 years later. Either I'm just that memorable or I keep coming up next on the "girls to recycle" list I swear all of these men (and women) have stashed away for a rainy day.

Thank you Luis for another lesson learned and more good times had. In the years before you, I probably would have stuck around despite realizing we had nothing in common and feeling uneasy with the situation, but I'm glad tides were turning and we were able to part ways amicably.

No Closer to Love

And those are the highlights (again, I use that word lightly) of my first foray into dating as a full-fledged adult in Miami which don't even begin to cover all of the other dates, short-lived entanglements, and complicated friendships that all ultimately let me down, too. Overall the problem seemed to be this: I couldn't connect with anyone I met in any real way. I could only do so sexually and on the surface with cheap laughs and good times that never turned into anything else. And the few times that a connection of some sort did form, it wasn't enough to sustain a real relationship due to misaligned interests and timing.

So (for that and many, many other reasons) I packed my bags and headed northwest in the hopes of something deeper. Little did I know the madness that awaited me.

Because, sure, I *did* find deeper connections in Chicago, but what I gained in depth I lost in sanity and honesty.

CHAPTER 5
Chicago's Not-My-Man Epidemic
and the Lesbian Confusion, Parts 1 and 2

There's a thin line between love, lust, and lies.

Part 1: Chicago's Not-My-Man Epidemic

The four years I spent in Chicago were truly some of the best years of my life for so many different reasons. And it wasn't because everything was perfect or because I didn't experience my fair share of heartache and confusion there. Rather Chicago is the first place where I felt totally and completely free to be me; to explore every piece of my being, even the super complicated, sometimes socially unacceptable bits.

For whatever reason, between the ages of 26 and 29, Chicago was my sanctuary, my evolution, my freedom—the place where I finally buckled down and faced every ugly, scary insecurity that had been spreading through me like wildfire my whole life—all of those things that had been too hard to face up until then. Those things that made me insecure, clouded my judgment, brought fear into my heart, and constantly whispered, "You are broken. You will never be fully worthy."

Sneaky Snake Tye

My Chicago journey through love began a month and a half after I moved there. I was rooming with an old college friend, working on my MBA, and soon after interning and working when I met Tye.

It was a chilly October night in ethics class (oh the irony!). The first time he spoke to me, I felt as though my words were trapped in my throat, attempting to swim up and make their way out but completely stalled by the, "DAMN. DAMN. DAMN!" of this man's fineness—he was definitely "forgive him fine," as my girl Lisa would say.

The epitome of tall, dark, and handsome, I swear his eyes twinkled as he spoke. That night we exchanged fiery glances and some small talk, and I left class walking on what felt like literal clouds. "This is it," I thought. All I had to do to find *him* was come to Chicago, and there he'd be, waiting for me, like something out of a fairytale. Oh young, naïve Sonia. She was real cute, y'all. Real, real cute.

In addition to the ethics class we had together, Tye and I had statistics together on Saturday mornings (Saturday morning class *and* math? Brutal, right?!). He'd always say hi with a huge ear-to-ear smile and that take-me-now twinkle in his eyes, but one Saturday he came ready to make a bigger move.

During break, he asked if he could talk to me outside for a second, and so, with my knees buckling from sheer excitement and nerves, I followed him out the door. That's when he laid it all out on me, or so I thought. He showed me a photo of what looked like a newborn baby—maybe just a couple months old—and said "Listen, I'm going to be real with you. I'm in the middle of a divorce, and we just had a baby, but I would really like to take you out on a date."

Hmmm. How refreshing, I thought. Sure, this was a complicated situation, especially for a 26-year-old who had just moved across the country and was beginning to settle into herself, but he seemed so honest and genuine. How could I discount him for his past when he was being this upfront with me—handing me his situation and asking me to take it or leave it? I was definitely impressed, so almost immediately, I said yes.

We made our plan to visit (yet another) Dave & Buster's in downtown Chicago soon after our sobering conversation outside statistics class. What can I say? It was magical. We were bouncing off of each other like toddlers on a sugar high. And although we had only known one another for a few weeks, it felt more like we'd been friends forever.

Tye was sexy (so damn sexy!), smart, fun, strong, and loving—yes, already—and I was on cloud nine, 10, and 11. Everything I had trouble finding in Miami had been placed right in my lap so easily that it almost felt like actual universe magic; like fate.

That night he took me home, said he had a great time, kissed me goodbye, and did not ask to come in—wow—this had only happened to me once or twice before, and it felt really, really nice. Over the course of the next few weeks, Tye and I shared moments, meals, and laughs. He sent me some music he had been working on, told me about his family, and opened up to me like a flower to a bee.

He told me about his years as a Chicago cop before he switched courses and decided to pursue his graduate degree in business. He'd seen a lot of horrible things during that time. He'd also gone through the tragic passing of his little brother. I started to understand him better.

Tye and I could be seen all over our business school campus stealing kisses and hugs and exchanging those passionate looks that kept me reeling with anticipation for days. And, despite all of the intensity between us, he wouldn't sleep with me. He said he wasn't ready, and, keeping his divorce situation in mind, I respected that, despite the fact that it was *incredibly* hard to not give in to the urge to literally jump his bones.

Then came the night that spiraled me into some significantly irresponsible and destructive behavior. I walked into the last session of our third class together—some online advertising elective—and saw a wedding ring flash at me from the other side of the room like lightning to the ground.

When I confronted him about the ring, crushed and beyond confused, he responded calmly, "My wife and I are getting back together. I told you that." Um, he most certainly had never, ever told me that, and I don't think that's something I would have forgotten. No sir. But that was his answer, and he didn't even squirm as he spit that pure-lie-laced-bomb out of his mouth and onto my horrified face.

My mind started spinning. Had the ring been there this whole time, and I just hadn't seen it? Was that possible? Had he been conveniently hiding it under his winter gloves when we'd meet outside to sneak a kiss in-between classes? Did she know about me? Had someone seen us *and* the ring? "Oh my God!" I thought. My classmates had seen me parading with this man all over campus. Did they know? What would they think of me now? How could he do this to me?

As it turns out, all of that upfront "honesty" had been a total sham. He hadn't even given me the opportunity to decide whether I wanted to be involved in such an affair, and now I looked like a complete whore. Needless to say I was *mortified*. Sure, in my younger, wilder years, I may have been with several not-so-single men, but married? Never. I know it doesn't make it better, but to me, that seemed like a whole different ball game I had never signed up to play. No ma'am.

Unfortunately Tye's initial deceit sent me into a tailspin of epically decadent proportions. I'm not proud of what comes next, but hear me out. I'd just been completely blindsided. I felt like a damn fool—one who never got a choice in the situation she suddenly found herself in. I felt small, more insecure than ever, betrayed by my instincts, and just plain mad as hell.

So I took an unorthodox approach to my healing by becoming the other woman in two different, but equally scandalous, situations. That's not to say that I purposely went out in search of these less than morally desirable situations—but I sure did use my pain to justify them once I'd given in.

I was not going to play the fool again, I thought. I was going to choose the situation I was in, and I was going to be the one in the know. I was not going to be blindsided again. I was going to have a good time, give in to every hot-blooded urge, and essentially be all kinds of terrible.

My Married Boyfriend

That same night, our entire class went to a bar to do our final presentations (yes, our professor was a unique gal). I got up shaking, knowing what I now knew and having to do this presentation with Tye sitting right there in my damn face, staring at me and smiling as if nothing at all had just gone down.

But I got through it, and the minute I was done, I headed straight to the bar. That's when one of my other classmates, Jake, started chatting me up. And three to four beers deep, after the entire class had already left the bar, I began to spill my guts to him. He was sweet, funny, and exactly the comfort I needed at that moment. One problem: he, too, was married. Although he wasn't trying to hide it, speak of some fake divorce, or anything like what Tye had done.

Honestly, at first, I just took our conversation as an innocent flirtation that would end as soon as last call came. But when he offered to take me home so I wouldn't have to take a bus drunk at that hour, things quickly got complicated. God, I was so naïve in those days. It almost makes me sick to think how blind I was when it came to men.

"He'll just get me home safe and sound, and that will be that. What a nice guy," I thought. And I'm not here to tell you that Jake wasn't a nice guy, because he was the sweetest, nicest man. But he was also a confused man who didn't know what he wanted and was too scared to try to find out.

As you may have guessed by now, when we got to my apartment, he asked if he could come up for a second to use the bathroom. At that point, I did start to get nervous. But he lived far outside the city, and I didn't want to make him drive the 45 or so minutes home about to pee his pants, so I let him up.

When he was done, he wanted to smoke a cigarette before heading out, so we walked back to the balcony and talked for a bit. And there it was, the moment I later realized he had been planning all night. In one awkward second or two, he blurted out how beautiful he thought I was and kissed me.

My pain over Tye kept me clamped to Jake's lips, even though, at the pit of my stomach, there was a voice screaming, "What the hell are you doing right now?!" I pretended not to hear it as we made our way to my bedroom and knowingly did a terrible, but still incredibly satisfying, thing.

Eastern European, short, and dorky (but still very cute!), Jake was the complete antithesis of Tye, except that he too was not mine to have. But at least with him, I knew from the get-go. Over the next couple of weeks, our affair progressed at an intensity I could have never imagined.

We'd go to dinner after class, enjoy delicious drinks, and laugh. God, we laughed so much. And every night we hung out, he'd drive me home and enthrall me in the kind of passion I'd only experienced from big, strong, beautiful black men. But it wasn't just the passion that sucked me in. It was also the tenderness with which he devoured my body and explored my mind.

Soon, in an extremely strange turn of events, Jake became the best "boyfriend" I had ever had. He always did what he said he was going to do. He checked in on me often and opened up to me with the same consistency. He showed me a good time and always got me home safe, even though it was insanely out of his way. And unlike most of the men of my past, he made me cum over and over again, no matter how long it took or how many mountains he had to move to make it happen.

Jake was also honest with me about his situation at home, or at least I think he tried to be. He told me that his wife had cheated on him, and things had never been the same after. He said he felt inadequate and stuck, but he loved her and was afraid to lose her. He explained that I made him feel good about himself and helped him forget all of his troubles—even if only for a little while. I lifted him up while being at home mostly brought him down.

There were so many times I told him that if he was unhappy and really wanted to leave, he should give himself a chance at joy again. He should just do it, I said, and not for me, because I wasn't trying to claim him *at all*, but for himself. Because it hurt me to see him spin out and struggle to lift himself out of the weight of his guilt while still yearning to feel something more, perhaps whatever it was he felt with me.

But Jake never listened to me. He said I didn't understand—his wife was his world. There was family involved (although no kids). A house. A mortgage. A history. And maybe he was right. I had never been married. I have no idea what it takes to make a marriage work and can't begin to understand why people stay when they're unhappy enough to go out and find joy in the streets, rather than at home with their significant other.

But one thing I've never understood is why a person would choose to deny himself a chance at real happiness. Why he would chose to crush his soul over and over again in a marriage that he basically admitted had him clawing at mental and emotional survival on a daily basis. And hey, maybe that's why I'm still single, who knows. I'm not one to stick around when I'm unhappy, feel unappreciated, or experience consistent pain—and that goes for cities, family, friends, jobs—all of it. I'm not a tree, and therefore I tend to pick up my things and move along with the feet and free will God gave me.

But to this day, as far as I know, Jake and his wife are still together, and according to social media, they look happy, and I'm happy for them. Truly. If they were able to find their way back to each other after all the cheating and pain, God bless. Maybe that's what a real marriage looks like. Maybe that's what it takes sometimes to get to the other side—a little destruction and mayhem to force two people into realizing what they really want and who they really want to be with.

As far as Jake and I go, about three months into our affair, we realized we were falling in love, and that's when we knew things had to stop. Immediately. Cold turkey. No more. And it was sad to let him go. Despite the unideal situation, he had made me happier than most men in my past had. In another life, at another time, there could have been something more between us. But alas, he was not for me but instead meant to be a small slice of my story—a slice I remember fondly and, dare I say, do not regret.

Sure, we ended up having a couple awkward run-ins at school, especially when we ended up working on the same team for a big, group term project. We argued about him not doing enough to contribute, and we exchanged some loud, strong words in the heat of the moment, but that was part of the tension and feelings that still boiled between us. I have no bad blood for Jake whatsoever and truly hope he is exceptionally happy. That's the funny thing about relationships; there are those from which all you can remember are the bad things and those from which all you can remember is the love, laughter, and orgasms. Thank you for those Jake. Seriously. Wow.

Thank you for making me feel special and loved at a time when I needed it most. Our situation was no fairy tale—that's for sure—but I think it fed us both in unique ways, and hopefully, it moved us closer to our truth, too.

Dan the Not-So-Man Man

After Jake, I still hadn't gotten the Tye-induced destruction out of my system, and I ended up in a more horribly inappropriate entanglement that honestly makes me sick in the gut to even think about, so I'll keep this one short and sweet.

Dan had a classic American boy-next-door look and worked at the same place I interned. He came on to me early in my time there, and he came on strong. I didn't even know what hit me for a while. He was one of the few white men to ever show me that kind of attention, and my insecure young, brown self didn't know what to do with it. I was creeped out and flattered all at the same time.

I actually did try to resist. This whole poorly thought out taken-man-revenge-plot of mine had grown tiresome and defeating, and I was trying desperately to change course. But after incessant pressing, I gave in to him a few times.

There was no sweetness or real connection with Dan, just his fetishized (he loved to rave about my Latin woman-ness) lust clawing at me for a cheap thrill. He told me he actually liked me and cared about me and would want to date me if he wasn't married, but I never felt any of that was true.

Honestly, with Dan I always felt somewhat manipulated and mind-fucked into the debauchery. Things never felt as voluntary as they had with Jake and the other not-so-single (but definitely not married) flames of my past.

After I got a urinary tract infection that a nurse suggested was likely caused by Dan removing the condom sometime during the act and our bacteria having a negative reaction to each other, my distaste for the whole situation only grew.

I was also bothered that Dan never showed any guilt whatsoever. He really and truly thought that cheating on his wife was not a big deal.

And although I did continue to respond to his messages for a while after the internship ended (I have such a problem ignoring people, but I'm working on it!), I only gave in to him maybe three times during the entire ordeal. And whenever he'd reach out, I'd promptly ask him about his wife and kids in case he thought, for one second, that I'd forgotten who he was.

Thankfully after enough attempts to ever-so-lightly blow him off, Dan left me alone. And even though it grosses me out to think about our physical interactions and his general abuse of power, I'm thankful to Dan for helping me wake up, so to speak.

After him I knew it was time to end the not-my-man retribution tour and work on being a better person. He made me realize that I'm better than that; I didn't want to be *that* person. I don't want to be someone who hurts people I don't even know, and I definitely want to have more respect for myself than giving in to his sick antics proved.

It's almost like I regained consciousness and started to slowly come back to myself. That's when I promised myself I'd never (knowingly) sleep with a married or otherwise taken man again. Plenty of them have tried over the years, but I stayed strong. I continued to lose my faith in men and marriage over those years, but at least I held on to my self-respect. That was worth more than anything.

Still, almost like an alcoholic with vodka, I did recently have one slip (after more than six years not-my-man sober!), and promptly after, I did little more than pray for forgiveness and promise to never, ever give in to it again, no matter how tempting the situation. Man, I never felt worse than after that night, because this time, I knew better. I've learned to forgive myself, though, and remember how well I've done at keeping the demons at bay all these years. I slipped and fucked up. I'm standing up and starting all over again.

And here's the thing that frustrates me to no end about all of this: every time I said no, did it change the fact that those individuals were seeking (very arduously, may I add) an affair? Each time it's happened, I've been 100%

single and not hiding from anyone. Yet so often, as a woman, I'm the one who receives the brunt of the blame, when I definitely only deserve half. But I guess that's the patriarchy hard at work once again!

For now, I'm going to focus on how I can continue to be and do better and remember that I can't control other people. And I certainly can't be responsible for their lies. I'm just so relieved I got this whole treacherous mess (mostly) out of my system when I did.

Thanks Dan for leading me closer to the light. It's really the only thing I'm thankful to you for.

Sneaky Snake Tye, Take II

Although I gladly never saw Jake or Dan again, Tye did manage to pull me into his mania a few more times over the next couple years, even when I moved to New York. After Jake and Dan, and everything in-between, I would see Tye around school and be friendly. He had reached out and apologized for his behavior, and told me he was still having trouble with his marriage. I decided to forgive him, because a part of me felt like he could use some sort of break to his tailspin of sadness and overall life complexity.

We'd share a friendly meal or conversation from time to time, but that was it. I even met his family at graduation and took photos with him. Weird, I know. I can't explain why I used to be able to forgive and forget so easily. Maybe I didn't have the energy to hold on to the hate and have always empathized, albeit a little too much, with people's imperfections. I guess it's because I've always been keenly aware of my own issues and shortcomings and tend to offer others the kind of understanding I often crave yet rarely get.

After graduation we lost touch until he reached out over LinkedIn (strange choice!) a few years later, and we got to talking. I had already left Chicago for New York, which he was surprised to learn, because he had left Chicago too—for Baltimore, just a three-hour ride from me.

He told me he was officially divorced but still close to his ex and had a second child with her. We reminisced about our history and the undeniable fire that had burned between us despite the complexity of our entanglements and the fact that we had never engaged in any physical activity past a passionate kiss or sweet handhold. Gradually we started to make our way back to each other over phone calls and texts.

Tye seemed to have matured and worked through a lot of his issues, plus having moved clear across the country away from his ex-wife (although he still went back to Chicago every month to see his boys), I felt like they were really done this time—at least romantically. He told me they worked better as friends and co-parents than as a married couple, and I thought it was awesome that they had found a healthy middle ground for their family. He seemed freer and happier than ever before, and I figured all that progress and change would make him a little saner too.

Before I knew it, I was on a bus to Baltimore to spend the weekend with him. I knew very well it might all crash and burn faster, louder, and stronger than the first time, but something in me couldn't walk away—not without giving it a real chance. For better or worse, I was still the hopeless romantic I'd always been; the girl who wanted to believe these crazy paths could one day lead to an amazing, movie-like love story.

We had a wonderful time that weekend. The simplest things brought us joy and connection: going grocery shopping, seeing a movie, sharing crab cakes, taking a midafternoon walk on the boardwalk, holding hands, and going for a run.

And guess what? We *still* didn't sleep together. Not because I didn't want to. Trust me, I was so frustrated I swear I contracted blue balls, no balls and all. We messed around and took things further than they had ever gone before, and I was sure it would happen, but he was *not* giving in. As his eager lips made their way from one thigh to the other and in-between, I thought OK, this is it. It's happening. Nope! JK, he said!

OK, he didn't really say JK, but that's what I heard when he insisted that we couldn't have full-on sex as he rose from between my legs smiling like a cartoonish fool saying, "I can't believe I'm going down on Sonia," as if I weren't in the room and in his mouth. I begged for a bit, but he insisted that he was too emotional a person to have sex outside a relationship and needed more time (as if it had not already been at least five years since we first met).

Then he told me he loved me, and I froze. It's not that I didn't have a million feelings pumping in my heart for him, it's more that I was having a hard time believing him, especially in such an intimate setting with such a big, serious declaration.

But fine, I accepted his reasons or excuses—whatever they were—and we went on with our still-great weekend. We said our goodbyes that Sunday at the bus stop, and it felt like this could be real this time around. I was satisfied (despite the blue balls), hopeful, and happy. And before I left his apartment, I left a note on his nightstand that said, "I do love you. I always have. I'm just scared."

He was happy to find it later that day, and for the next week we'd text and chat, reminiscing about our beautiful weekend together and admiring how far we'd come from our troubled past. We couldn't wait to see each other again.

But we never would. It wasn't long (at all) before Tye started to act erratic and began to argue with me for no reason. One day, we had a big argument about God knows what (I can't remember for the life of me), and a distinct sense of déjà vu crept up, reminding me who I was dealing with. Basically, I think he got scared again, and wanted any reason to run away, so I let him. I was upset that it had all come crashing down so quickly, but I was also strangely calm.

I got over Tye in about a week that time around. I was proud of myself for being open to second chances and taking the trip to Baltimore to see what was or wasn't there. Giving it a shot, with an open heart and mind, was the right thing for me to do, and I still remember that weekend fondly. Nothing changes the fact that we had a dazzling time together, during which we shared many sweet, intimate, and refreshing moments. It's almost as if we had been an official couple for those few short days, and I didn't regret it for one moment.

But alas, it was time to accept, once and for all, that Tye was not a mentally healthy man. He lived somewhere between fantasy and reality, and he had a lot of work to do. Most importantly, none of it had a thing to do with me. Maybe he wanted to love me but found himself too trapped by his own demons to do so successfully. And I wish him the best. It's been about three and a half years now, and I hope he's battling those demons less today. I also hope his kids are well and he's found some semblance of happiness. But I'm still glad he's out of my life forever. I gave him every chance I had in my bones to give.

Thank you Tye for helping me grow in ways I never knew I needed to. Thank you for opening up a different, more forgiving, and more understanding part of myself. Thank you for never allowing us to become just another notch on the ol' bedpost. And thank you for *trying* to love me in the best way you knew how. Whenever I think of you, I'll try to focus on that and not on all the pain and absurdity that traveled between us.

PART II: The Lesbian Confusion

My foray into the great lesbian confusion of 2012 didn't start in Chicago. It goes all the way back to my first year in college, exactly a decade before.

Growing up I was always a little more than boy crazy. In fact, I was fairly known for it to the tune of, "Oh God, who is she crying over or writing a poem about now?" But when I was 17 and went away to college with my best friend from high school, something strange, new, and wonderful happened; I fell in love with her (while I was still very much with Luca!).

We started college during the summer term and moved into an apartment-type dorm with four bedrooms. There was one other girl and an empty room. My friend Ivy and I got two adjacent bedrooms. And at first, things were normal between us, just like they'd always been. But the more she began to hang out and sleep over in my tiny dorm room in this new, scary, and exciting place, the more something started to shift.

Ivy's parents had decided to wait until the fall semester to buy her a computer and TV, so she'd hang out in my room all the time to use mine (kinda funny how the poor girl had more stuff!). And it was fun. Of course it was fun—she was my best friend, and after growing up in strict homes, we now had this perpetual sleepover six hours away from our parents. What's not to love?

I'm not saying we developed feelings for each other because we were hanging out in the same room a lot—it doesn't quite work like that. The setup merely allowed for whatever might have been there all along, hiding deep in our subconscious, to find its way to the surface.

At first we had flirty interactions here and there. She used to do this "nosies" thing where she'd rub my nose with hers and ask me, "Who's your little pacific islander?" which I later realized didn't make any sense because she was from Trinidad, but that's beside the point! At first she would do it occasionally when we were alone, but then she started doing it in front of other friends, and that's when I was like, "OK, I'm not crazy, right? She *is* coming on to me, correct?"

That was just the beginning. Sometimes we'd be lying in bed having what I first thought was just an innocent sleepover between friends, when she'd say, "Hey, I have a fun idea! Why don't we take our shirts off?" Um OK! Clearly, although I didn't really understand what was happening or what I was feeling, I was into it. And I felt free to explore it, because when I told Luca what was happening, he just laughed. I guess he wasn't threatened, although he should have been. That's ignorance for ya!

Things got real a few days before our 18th birthdays (just two days apart) when we tried to go to a club in downtown Gainesville. We figured we had technically already been alive for 18 years and the bouncers would let us in, but we couldn't have been more wrong.

So after getting all dressed up to go out for our special night on the town, we had to call my sister's boyfriend to come pick us up no more than 10 minutes after he had dropped us off. We'd been looking forward to our first night out at a club so much, so to cheer us up, he bought us beer and invited us to come sleep over at my sister's place where he was also staying, and where we would have more room to spread out and they could keep an eye on our drinking.

So we went back and drank our illicit beers on a big blanket on the floor of the living room, where we giggled and carried on until things got heated. The alcohol had stripped away both my fear and my deep lack of understanding for the feelings I was having for a girl—and not just any girl, but my best friend.

In a drunken stupor, I began to outline the v-shaped neckline on her dress with my fingers as I lay my head on her shoulder. We were talking softly as my fingers turned into lips, and although I was calm and nonchalant on the outside, on the inside I was screaming.

I looked up at her and caressed her face as I went in for a kiss, but that's when she stopped me. She said a kiss was too intimate and she wasn't ready for that step, which left me completely confused because I'd just had her bare breast in my mouth a couple seconds before.

I cried, partially from the rejection and partially from the confusion. She said she was sorry and tried to comfort me, explaining that she'd never been with a man and she felt she had to take that step before she could go any further with me. Eventually we fell asleep in a sort of half-cuddled position, and when we awoke in the morning, we both looked at each other, trying to rub the sun out of our eyes with a look of, "Did that actually happen last night, or was it just a dream?"

After that night things intensified between us but also became more awkward. It's as if we were trying to figure out how to reconcile our friendship with this exciting romantic dynamic, and for the life of us, we couldn't do it. And listen, I completely understood every ounce of her hesitation. Even though I was more sexually and romantically experienced at the time, I was still confused and conflicted by my feelings for her. After all, I had a boyfriend back home who I was in love with and thought I might marry someday. But I was still trying to be open to the new feelings and explore them with honesty and transparency, something she didn't seem capable of doing.

When we were out and about, we were the Sonia and Ivy everyone knew, but behind closed doors we'd become something else. It's funny, because when I think about it, Ivy and I never actually had sex or even really kissed, yet somehow we had some of the most intense sexual moments I've ever had. Maybe it seemed so intense because it felt like we were doing something wrong or because we wouldn't let ourselves go past a certain point. She'd ask me to kiss her body but never let me kiss her lips. And it was always me doing the touching or kissing or nibbling. I guess I was OK with that. To feel close to her in some way was enough for me.

Unfortunately it wasn't long before things between us became too tense to handle. The more stressed out I saw her become about the feelings she couldn't handle, the more I tried to explain to her that we didn't *have* to be romantic. If she was that agitated by the situation, we could put it all behind us and go back to being friends only.

But who was I kidding? When the dynamic between two friends changes to that degree, it's nearly impossible to go back. Especially when it involves a new side of your sexuality laden with this weird shame you never even knew you'd feel until you were actually going through it and not in the role of someone else trying to reassure another that everything was going to be OK.

We began to argue about pretty much everything until I realized it simply wasn't working. I became increasingly frustrated because she made me feel like I was some big lesbian monster who was always coming on to her and making things difficult. I took high offense to that, because my number one priority had always been to respect her limits as we walked down this new path together.

There were many times when I was too afraid to even initiate anything, even though the sexual tension between us was sharp enough to cut through a brick. And every time she'd end up straight up *asking* me to make a move. Which was totally fine by me, but I didn't appreciate her insinuating that I pressured her whenever we got in an argument. I felt like she was trying to find an easy way out from feelings she couldn't accept and didn't want to deal with.

Eventually the circumstances ended our friendship. We tried to reconnect and even talked about (well, really she practically begged me, saying she wanted to get our friendship back on track) moving in together again for our sophomore year, but when I came back from a weekend in Miami visiting Luca, she had signed a lease with two of my friends (MY friends!). In the meantime, I had said no to several people who had offered to room with me and was left scrambling to find a roommate. In hindsight, I guess it wasn't the worst thing in the world, but back then it felt like a huge betrayal. I've never been one to take people's word lightly, and I trusted her to maintain our verbal contract.

In the years that followed, I remained friends with her roommates, who hadn't realized she had promised to live with me, and so she was sort of around, but mostly I avoided her at all costs. She'd ask my friends about me often and say she wished we could be friends, but I was done.

I heard things about her here and there, but never actively kept up with her life. I actually ran into her at the supermarket in Miami in 2017, nearly hitting her with my cart. When I realized it was her, I peeled off in the other direction like a crazy person. It's been a long time, and I have no hard feelings, but if I had stopped to say hi, would she treat me like the big scary lesbian she had treated me like all those years ago? I was definitely not interested in finding out.

After Ivy, I had crushes on girls here and there, even on some of my friends (which we would be totally open about and laugh about all the time), but I could never work up the nerve to do anything about it. And every time I felt like I got close to summoning the gumption to talk to a girl or flirt with one, I would look around and suddenly feel so exposed that all I could do was retract back into my shell like a scared turtle in a crowd.

And honestly, I was still so boy crazy, that I thought it was probably OK to ignore that part of myself. It wasn't until I was 28 years old and living in Chicago—what I lovingly call the gayest city in the world—that I really began to explore that side of me again. Most of my friends in Chicago were gay men. Being around them, hanging out where they hung out, and seeing how free they were finally made me feel comfortable enough to face those feelings when they arose. Thanks boys! Love you. Mean it.

That's when I met Isabella, but she went by Isa. I never called her that, though. I loved the femininity of her name and the way it rolled off my tongue and through my ears. I've never been one for nicknames, anyway. I have this thing about wanting to call people by their full beautiful names, and, most of the time, they put up with it.

She was a barista at the Starbucks across the street from where I went to school in the evenings in downtown Chicago, and every time I saw her, my knees quite literally felt weak and my stomach filled with so many butterflies it felt as though they could fly out of my mouth at any moment and blow my cover.

I can vividly picture her smile—a great big beaming smile she'd give me as she handed me my nightly cup of coffee and I tried to keep my spaghetti-weak legs from dropping me straight to the floor. There was definitely a spark there, but could she really be into me, or was she just doing her job? One night I decided I had to find out once and for all.

It was summer 2012, and I was two weeks away from completing my last class for my **MBA**. That meant I'd no longer have a reason to go to that particular Starbucks, and if I didn't make my move then, I might never know what could have been, or worse yet, I'd probably never see her again. I couldn't bare it. Not this time. I had a crush on a girl, and I was going to give myself the space and freedom to face that.

So I wrote my name and phone number on a little piece of paper, and I carved out my plan. After enough encounters, I had more or less figured out the time she usually took her break, so I planned to arrive then. I didn't want to approach her while she was actually working, especially since I was likely going to be a whole hell of a hot mess, so I figured a quiet, more private moment outside would be much better, even if it only resulted in lemon-sour rejection.

And sure enough, when I arrived with my perfectly estimated timing, she was sitting on the sidewalk across from the restaurant smoking a cigarette. So I walked over and asked if I could sit down and talk to her for a moment. With a huge smile of intrigue on her face and that all-too-familiar sparkle in her eyes, she kindly obliged. And with the fear of a thousand wars in my gut, I proceeded to explain myself.

I told her I was "straight" and had never approached a girl in this way, but I felt like there was something there, and before I finished school and never saw her again, I had to know if she felt the same. Was I imagining the fireworks between us, or was there something there? And without hesitation, she confirmed there was. So I proceeded to ask her if we could hang out sometime. I couldn't even believe the words as I heard them vibrating off my tongue and into the world, but there I was for the first time, facing my fears and asking a girl out.

To my delighted surprise, it went better than I ever imagined, and she was totally into it. So we said our goodbyes, and I headed off to class. It wasn't even an hour later before she was texting me to grab a drink that night as I sat in class trying to contain the big goofy smile on my face and keep my legs from dancing back across the street to Starbucks. What I didn't know when I joyfully accepted her immediate invitation was just how wildfire-complicated things were about to get.

When we got to the bar that night, there was an instant closeness. And even though I'd never been out with a girl like this, I felt at ease. Maybe it helped that we were in a tiny gay bar all the way on the other side of town from school.

We sat across from each other on bar stools with my legs nestled comfortably between hers, chatting and laughing like we had known each other for much longer than just a few hours. I could feel the blood rushing through my veins and was smiling so hard I could have easily popped a blood vessel. At that moment, it felt like there was nothing and no one else in the room—just me and her in that bar, sitting at the cusp of passion and in the midst of a revolution.

That's when she began to tell me about the "complicated" relationship she was in. Apparently she lived with the woman, but they'd break up almost every other day. Basically she was trying to be honest with me and let me know she came with some drama, as if to warn me or give me the opportunity to walk away. But I was entranced, and much like I often did at that messy time in my life, I charged on. Hey, she wasn't married, right?

That same night we went home together. She lived in Indiana, about an hour outside of Chicago and it had gotten pretty late, so she shyly (or maybe slyly) asked if she could stay with me, and even though I was a little hesitant (because I didn't know this girl from Adam), I was too excited to jump into this new, exciting feeling to say no. Luckily she didn't murder me. She only broke my heart.

So off we went. I'm not sure I've ever been quite so nervous. As a more experienced gay woman, Isabella, I assumed, would make the first move and guide the conversation of our bodies so I wouldn't have to. But it was clear she had a crush and she was just as, if not more, nervous than me. I honestly think she was trying to be respectful and err on the side of extreme caution because I was sort of an in-between as far as my sexuality went. So after enough dilly dallying, I had to get blunt about what I wanted to happen. It was terrifying and exhilarating.

As she took my direction/permission and proceeded to slowly position her body on top of mine, she pressed her lips softly against mine with our eyes meeting at the same time. My whole body began to scream with a raging, tingling sensation so all-consuming that I'm fairly certain I forgot my name for a moment. After that, our bodies entangled themselves so naturally and effortlessly it was impossible to not completely surrender to that little part of me that had been there all along, patiently waiting to announce itself, for the 10 long years between the first time I realized I had strong feelings for a girl (Ivy) and the first time I found myself actually sleeping with one (Isabella).

It was like a dream; so different from anything I could have ever imagined or expected, but more beautiful than anything I could have ever hoped for. But sure enough, that perfect night in that perfect trance quickly (too quickly!) turned into a whirlwind romance that left me reeling and asking for mercy in a matter of weeks.

There was also the added layer of my deepening confusion. If I was really a lesbian, wouldn't I have figured it out long before my late 20s? And how could I have been so totally boy crazy all those years?

From then on, Isabella began staying over to the point that it felt like she had practically moved in. And she had drama, drama, drama with her on and off girlfriend. Unfortunately I was entrenched in the painful naiveté of trying to create something and be something that we would never have and never be.

Still there was a spark and an infatuation that kept us playing our losing game. Every time I saw her, no matter how mad or annoyed I might have been with her five minutes before, her sexy smile, sparkly eyes, and intoxicating scent were always enough to make me forget everything—suddenly losing all ability to think about anything other than reaching for her lips—man those were a good pair of lips!

But that haze of emotion wasn't enough to stop our ultimate demise. It probably wasn't even a month before things had become way too intense that I started getting tired of feeling more like her mother than her lover. Isabella was a lost bird, and I didn't have the patience or ability to save her. She didn't want to be saved, either. She also turned out to be more of a dog than any man I'd ever known. Go figure.

So off she went, back to Indiana and her dysfunctional relationship that continued to fall apart like clockwork at least once a week. I was heartbroken and confused, but part of me was also relieved. I missed her and ached for her like we'd been together for years, but alas, that's just the way my heart works. It rarely, if ever, loves lightly, irrespective of time.

Over the course of the next three years or so, Isabella and I would come back to each other many times, but we never tried to pretend again. I'd seen who she was and she'd seen who I was, and we knew there could be nothing more between us than friendship and occasional lust. But that doesn't mean it wasn't complicated. The feelings we once had for each other always lingered, and tensions between my good-girl tendencies and her bad-girl ones were always boiling right at the surface of every interaction.

I was also frustrated with Isabella's insistence on being a general mess at life. I knew she could do better, and I wanted better for her, but I couldn't help someone who didn't want to be helped. Once she told me she needed me in her life because I was the only positive influence she had, and I was honored to be that for her, if only she would actually listen to me. She was a smart, charismatic, funny, and clever woman, yet she insisted on slacking off; moving from job to job, girl to girl, and home to home; and getting into fights, among other things. She seemed lost and unhappy but insistent on not changing.

During one particularly heated conversation, I told her, "You grew up in a middle-class home in the suburbs of Illinois. You had love and means and were given every opportunity, but you insist on wanting to be this big gangster. I grew up on welfare, yes with love, but with little means, and I make no excuses. I've gone out and made it for myself, and I can't for the life of me understand why you complain and call me lucky. You can do anything I've done. You can do anything you want. But until you work on keeping yourself out of trouble and away from the wrong crowd, nothing is ever going to change."

And listen, I'm no one to tell anybody how to live their lives. But don't come to me and tell me I'm "lucky" when I've worked my ass off for every little thing I have and for every opportunity I've been afforded. No one ever *gave* me anything. I had to go out and get it; fight for it. So when someone tells me they want better for themselves too, all I ask is that they leave the jealousy at the door and get up and do something. That's all I'm saying.

Had Isabella been happy in her life, I would've let her be. But that's what happens when you love someone and they come to you with their problems. You try to offer them love, advice, and the help they're supposedly seeking. That is, of course, until you realize they have zero intention of accepting any of it.

The last time I saw Isabella was during one of my visits to Chicago after I moved to New York City in early 2015. I'd seen her before on my previous trips back, but we'd always kept it platonic; drinks, conversation, the inevitable flirtation, and nothing more. But this time, I missed her in a different way, and I wanted to share a bed with her again—even if just for old times' sake.

In my then "old" age (30, that is), I didn't want any kind of trouble, so the first thing I did was reach out and ask if she was single, to which she responded that she was. Of course I should've known better, but I trusted her response anyway. Maybe I just ached for her that bad. So I told her I wanted to see her and *be* with her during my trip. I asked her if she was up for it, and she didn't hesitate for one second to engage in my proposal.

The day I arrived, she met up with me at a restaurant, where we had lunch and a couple drinks. After that we headed back to my friend's house that I'd been staying at; no one would be home from work for a while. I think she was living with her mom in the suburbs at the time, and a last-minute hotel seemed unnecessarily expensive, so I braved the thought of taking her back to my friend's place.

I figured I'd ask for forgiveness rather than permission. I was staying in the guest room during my visit, so I figured I'd wash the sheets before I went home, and no biggie. Luckily my friend, who did find out later, thought it was hilarious that I actually tried to tell him we just took a nap together. His partner found it funny too. What can I say? I am a terrible, terrible liar. I was so relieved they were amused and not upset—you're the best, guys!

Being with Isabella that day was everything I'd been yearning for and more. It was like no time had passed since we had been intimate. And we were able to laugh at the fact that we were at this strange point in our relationship—basically two good friends who also liked to sleep together sometimes. Such a unique, wonderful dynamic that is with a girl! The best part was, just as we got started, my other friend showed up to visit. We'd made plans to meet up and I had lost track of the time with Isabella.

So we got up to let her in and sat with her in the living room for a bit trying our hardest not to let it show that we were dying to go back and finish what we'd started. That's when I decided to come clean with my friend and tell her what we were about to do when she called and said she was downstairs. I explained that I probably wouldn't get another chance to see Isabella again during that trip and asked if it'd be horrible for her to just hang out while we went back in the room and did our thing. God love her: she said, "Go, enjoy yourself!" while also laughing hysterically. Now that, ladies and gentleman, is a true friend—thanks boo!

A week or two after my trip, I was texting with Isabella about her coming to visit me in New York, and suddenly she dropped off the face of the earth. I gave it some time and reached out again. That's when I found out that she was not in fact single at the time of our Chicago rendezvous. She was with the same on and off girlfriend from years prior, who had looked through Isabella's phone while she was sleeping. The girlfriend had seen all our texts from the last couple weeks, and she was *mad*. Obviously.

For years Isabella had told her that I was straight and just a friend she'd met during her short time at college. The poor woman had always believed that and knew we hung out from time to time but never had a problem with it. One time she even picked up the phone to let me know Isabella was in the shower and would be heading out to meet me soon. Awkward.

After the girlfriend saw these texts, however, she realized for the first time in several years that Isabella and I had always been more than friends and proceeded to lose it—understandably so. I received nasty, homophobic (don't you love it when queer folks are homophobic because your queerness is different than theirs?) messages on Facebook during which she threatened to "expose" me on a small blog I was running at the time. Little did she know that I'm an open book who intentionally exposes herself all the time. Anyhow, once I blocked her, she sent her friends after me, who also slung homophobic comments my way and told me that I needed to decide whether I wanted a man or a woman. Not to mention called me disgusting over and over again.

It's interesting how when people cheat, no one ever wants to go after the cheater, the one who actually betrayed their trust. Instead they want to come after someone who can only go off the information she was given. I contacted Isabella and told her she needed to talk this woman down because their complete and total disrespect for each other and their relationship was not my problem. I also told her I don't deal with people this way, and I wasn't about to sit down and argue with this woman and her lowlife friends or defend myself, because I did nothing wrong.

I think Isabella must have talked to her and maybe promised to never speak to me again, because that's what happened and the girlfriend backed down. At the end of the day, Isabella finally broke up with that woman for good and is now married to someone else. We are connected on social media but rarely talk. I think I sent her a note of congrats when I saw she got married, and we've had a few interactions and texts here and there, but that's it. We actually tried to hang out the last time I was in Chicago, just for a quick bite, but it didn't work out, and I'm glad. As committed as I am to not involving myself in any more madness, we probably can't be trusted alone together. And I'm so done with all the drama. It's not worth the trouble.

I do think about Isabella all the time and hold no ill will against her whatsoever, as I hope she does for me. In fact I'm forever thankful to her for opening me up to a side of myself I'd kept in the shadows for so long. I'm thankful that she helped me figure out that I'm not a lesbian or straight, but queer, and that's OK. She showed me how to be open to a different kind of passion, a different kind of friendship, and a different kind of love.

She also made me laugh and shake (the good kind!) uncontrollably. She taught me patience. She gave me memories I will cherish forever. She taught me to be careful with girls' feelings if I'm not willing or able to be completely or seriously devoted to them. And, for whatever it's worth, I hope she is safe and happy and coming into her own as the woman I always knew she could be.

I know that I loved Isabella and she loved me, and that's good enough for me. But she knew I could never truly be with her. One thing that my journey with her made me realize is that, although I'm occasionally attracted to women and even have the capacity to fall in love with them, in the long-term, I want to be with a man. That's what feels comfortable and right for me, and that's OK. It's empowering to know where you stand.

I have to respect that truth and accept that, unless I found a woman on a similar path as me who could be comfortable with this truth, it's unfair to expect women to want to date me. That's why, until this day, I've never seriously pursued anything with a woman again. And with Isabella, I was always honest, even during that time when I wasn't completely sure of the truth I know now.

Unfortunately, we don't always hear what we're clearly being told but instead often only what we *want* to hear, and I might have hurt Isabella because of this. I hope she knows that was never my intention.

Thank you Isabella—for everything.

CHAPTER 6
Windy City Fuckboys

Sometimes love is just an idea, a wish, a yearning; nothing but a little reality and a lot of pretend.

Along with all the growth, confusion, and interesting-to-say-the-very-least years, my time in the Windy City (Chicago) also "gifted" me two of the biggest fuckboys I've ever known. On the bright side, they taught me so much about who I am, what I want, and what I deserve. Eric and Felix: names permanently burned in my brain like the typewriter tattoo inked onto my wrist.

Now I've already written an entire book on Eric (*My Funny, Sad Life: I Once Loved a Sociopath*—go check it out!), so I'll spare you those details again here. Suffice it to say that I still think about him almost every day (and have often snuck a peek at his social media, although I have recently committed myself to never looking again), but not in an I'm-not-over-him kind of way. It might have taken me a really, really long time (about five years), but I can now confidently say I am over Eric. Maybe I'm not over what he did to me or how he affected me, but I am over *him*. I do often think I never want to feel the kind of debilitating pain he caused me again, which definitely affects how I approach dating and love, but in time, I know that too will fade.

Eric is still very much a part of me, as he'll always be. I'm OK with that. Truly. He is a critical part of my puzzle, and I almost cherish that now-stale, but ever so relevant pain. At times I even manage to have a pleasant memory of that year we spent together and smile. What more could I ask for?

But Felix. Oh Felix. When I started writing this book, I honestly didn't think to include him, largely because we'd actively become friends after his move to Miami, where I currently live. But thinking about it now, how could I even begin to think about betraying the truth in that way? I guess even after everything I've been through, I'm still a sucker for love and second (and third and fourth) chances, and I can't deny the tragic beauty in that.

It's truly bizarre to me that a man (and I use the term quite loosely) I met through a dating website in Chicago in 2011 could end up living down the street from me in my hometown in 2017. Even more bizarre is how our past could manage to explode in our faces (well mostly in mine) yet one more time.

That's one lesson I still struggle to put into play, even after all the times I've been forced to relearn it: the past should be left in the past because, if given the chance at another act, the likelihood that it will repeat its ugly self is mind-numbingly real. And that's not to say that there aren't exceptions to the rule, because there always are, but I should know by now that my love luck doesn't like to travel in that direction.

Killjoy Boy Toy

I met Felix on OKCupid in 2011, when I was 26 years old. I was the heaviest I'd ever been (blame it on too many I-love-Chicago celebratory tacos and margaritas!), and I was hesitant to date, but I put myself out there anyway. Because, well, sometimes to my advantage and other times to my great disadvantage, I'm a stubborn optimist—or at least when it comes to love, I used to be.

Our first date was awkward but good, and it went on all day. We had brunch (during which I felt like he waited an eternity to pick up the check; I assume because he was waiting for me to offer to split it, even though it was only $30—AWKWARD!). Then we had *coquito* (that delicious coconut ice cream you buy from a little old man with a cart and scrape out of a hairy coconut shell that tickles your fingertips) on a park bench.

Later, as the day grew dark, we went back to my apartment to hang out for a while before he had to leave for a family party. A few hours after he left, he came back to bring me a plate of food from said party (that's so Felix—as sweet and giving as he is cluelessly cruel and cheap), and we hung out a little longer watching a movie and chit chatting.

Right away I thought Felix was cute and sweet, and obviously interested in me, but I was still hesitant—in my heart of hearts, something always felt off about him, but it was never anything I could actually pinpoint. From the beginning, though, I noticed he was a bit shy and conservative, which is basically the complete opposite of me. I was afraid I'd be too much for him (not that this Sonia-is-too-much phenomenon is particular to Felix in any way), and I'm not exactly the kind of girl who can turn down her shine. Anyway, why should I? Still, like so many other times in my confused life, there was something that drew me to him.

Felix seemed different from most of the guys I'd dated before; he was smart and sweet, and he liked to go on actual dates and try new things. So I gave it a shot. But somehow in a matter of only three or four weeks, things between us became explosive, and not in a fun, sexy way but in an ugly, combative, name-calling way.

Felix and I had a nice time together, but he could be exceptionally judgmental. It was almost enough to make my skin crawl with anxiety every time I saw or spoke to him. I could practically feel the dry pull of the tension in the air every time I drank a glass of wine (he wasn't much of a drinker), dared to speak of smoking a cigarette (which fine, I understand), became too chatty, or got a little lost driving (even a GPS isn't enough to keep me from getting lost sometimes!). Mind you, I was *always* the one driving because he didn't have a car, *but whatever.*

As I'd initially suspected he would, Felix always made me feel like I was *too much*. And, again, I'm no stranger to feeling like this, but it always felt more intense with him. The scent of disapproval was so thick that I almost felt like I could touch it. For him, I was too open, too sexual, too contentious, too strong, too everything. And it was making me feel *sick*.

One night, after we'd gone out dancing, he started to act super annoyed and frustrated with every move I made and word I said. At the end of the night, we went back to some aunt's house he'd been staying at (while she was away on vacation), where he suddenly became aggressive. He angrily asked me what we were doing and said that he felt weird because we were sleeping together but weren't officially together. Then he proceeded to tell me my feet smelled. (I hadn't been in Chicago long and hadn't quite gotten the hang of winter boot care. My bad!!!)

I was confused. Why was he *so* mad? We had only been seeing each other for a few weeks, and we were 26 years old, not 15. I told him we weren't boyfriend and girlfriend yet because he hadn't asked, we hadn't discussed it, and because that's just what adults do—they date and get to know each other, and yes, sometimes they sleep together and see where things go. The fight intensified to the point that I felt like I had to get out of there stat. So I grabbed all my stuff and went to my car. I sat there crying my eyes out, alone on a dark street somewhere in Evanston, Illinois, in the middle of the night.

After a few minutes he came outside and got in the car to talk to me. That's when I experienced the nastiest I'd ever had a man be to me outright, right to my face. He was cruel and callous, not to mention completely unhinged, as he proceeded to tell me that he was going to give me some advice to put into practice the next time I tried to date someone (I'm choking on the bitter taste of his atrocious arrogance even as I write this now).

And although I might not remember many specific details from those weeks I spent with Felix or from that night, I'll never, ever forget those words, or that hateful look on his face when he delivered those acid flames into my eardrum and down into my already-weakened heart. Are you ready for this? Brace yourself honey.

Felix looked me square in the eyes and explained (I mean, mansplained) that as a man, he was always going to make a move, but as a woman, it was my duty (yes, he said *duty*) to deny him. He also declared that the "availability" of sex had turned him off.

In complete shock, because, well, it was 2011, not 1925, and I had never in my entire life heard someone say something so vile, sexist, and completely disgusting (guess 2017 showed me!), I told him to get the fuck out of my car, which he did immediately. And as soon as that door closed, I drove off as fast as I possibly could. His hand may or may not have still been on the door handle at the time of takeoff (#sorrynotsorry).

I drove away enough to be out of his sight and had to pull over on the side of the road. I was in full panic-attack mode. I called my then-best friend in New York (bless her for being there for me that night), and she talked me down enough for me to regain a normal breathing pattern and be able to drive myself home, where I cried myself to sleep through the excruciating exhaustion and confusion of it all.

The next day, Felix and I texted a bit, and I unloaded on him. I reminded him that from the beginning, I'd let him know that I wasn't some princess or quaint, quiet yes-woman, and if that's what he was looking for, he should look elsewhere, because it wasn't me, nor was it ever going to be me. I told him to stop trying to put me in a box.

Then this man dared to take things even further than he already had the night before with his prehistoric, misogynistic, and truly repulsive mandates of how I, as a woman, should behave to retain his interest. He said that if he'd really been trying to put me in a box, he would've judged me about my weight (sounds like judgment to me!). Excuse me?

That's when I said something to the effect of, "How dare you? You're fat too!" to which he responded that he was at the grocery store and was so hurt that he couldn't feel his legs and had to sit down. I still laugh out loud every time I think of those words. Brotha please! So you can dish it, and dish it really good, might I add, but you can't take it? Get the fuck out of here with that foolishness.

When the conversation was over, I felt almost relieved that he had made himself so crystal clear with his outlandish behavior, which was not my problem to deal with. He obviously had some deep emotional issues to contend with, and all of this was nothing more than pure projection. So we parted ways, and I threw myself into weight loss like I'd never done before in my life. I wouldn't say that it was *all* about him, but he certainly played a role.

I felt appalled by Felix and his audacity, and at the same time, I felt a plea coming from within myself, begging me to do something to pick my self-esteem off of the floor, where it had been laid for me to step on over and over again. So I signed up for a personal trainer, and over the course of just four months, a lot of tears, and a partially Felix-driven need to rid myself of his poisonous touch and grotesque insults, I lost 50 pounds. (Ahhh, those all-too-brief days of thinness—what a magical time to be alive!)

I was completely celibate during that time and for several months after I lost the weight. Part of me still felt disgusted at the thought of giving my body to a man who would gladly devour it only to then insult it and degrade it the moment it no longer suited him. I still felt shy the first time I got naked with the next person I slept with, who I told about the incident. He was so sweet in that moment of weakness—he smiled and said that he wasn't *that guy,* and he loved what he saw.

Unfortunately, as I hinted at before, the grocery store knee-buckling telephone call wasn't the end of Felix and me. I know. I know. I'm truly the worst when it comes to this tragic romance recycling program.

Throughout the next couple of years, he'd reach out periodically, even after he went off to Michigan for graduate school, and subsequently to Haiti for a few years, while I eventually moved from Chicago to New York City and then back home to Miami. So many times during our conversations over the years he pleaded with me to forgive him for what he'd said and done during our brief affair in Chicago, promising that he didn't mean any of it and that he couldn't even understand why he had behaved that way. He also went on and on about how amazing I am and how much he admired me and my ability to be raw and open, something I swore he had heavily judged me for before. One time he even went as far as to say that he wished he could be more like me. MIND BLOWN.

And although I chose to forgive him and believe that he had truly matured and seen the error in his ways, I still could never truly take Felix seriously or shake the feeling that he continued to be a strange and deeply disturbed bird. More than that, while I sincerely tried to forgive, I could never, ever forget. He'd simply been too precise with his cruelty, too irresponsible with his words. Nevertheless I continued to entertain his attempts and conversations. Because let's be honest. That's just what Sonia does or *did*.

So maybe it follows that I was asking for what happened next. For years my gut diligently told me to just say no, but off I went time after time after time. And for several years, minus one time when he actually came over, most of our contact seemed innocent and safe enough because it primarily involved social media interactions and WhatsApp messages. That is until he decided to move to Miami in early 2017, where I had moved back to a few months prior.

Before he actually moved, Felix reached out to tell me he'd be in town for an overnight layover to Chicago and wanted to see me. This rendezvous involved me driving to an airport to pick him up that is a huge pain in the butt to get to late at night, *and* it was a school night. But, reservations and all, I said yes.

When the time to go meet him got close, I was tired and wanted to cancel, but something always calls my heart to things that feel dangerous or wild—what can I tell ya? We'll catch up and grab a bite, and I'll have a nice night out of the house, I thought. What's the big deal? We'd been chatting for a couple years on pretty friendly terms (although I did sense a hint of flirtation in the air), and he was unlikely to try anything. How bad of an idea could this really be?

And maybe it ended up being OK for that night, but the ginormous can of worms that blasted open in those few hours would end up having much more lasting repercussions—ones I am still dealing with today.

The second I picked Felix up, there was this giggly, nervous tension in the air. I guess sexual attraction is funny and resilient in that way. Often, no matter how much you believe an old flame has died, never to be felt or heard from again, there it always is, just waiting patiently to be given even the slightest chance to breathe again.

So off we went to a Mexican food spot to grab a bite, have a drink, and catch up. Upon arriving, we were quickly seated in a cozy little booth complete with dim lighting and Felix sitting so close to me that he might as well have sat right on my lap. Soon he had his hand on my thigh and his intentions dripping plainly from his goofy, sweet smile. I was taken aback by this unusual forwardness, but nevertheless, I welcomed it. I guess in the back of my head, I knew it was a possibility. Otherwise I wouldn't have been so nervous driving there that night, nor would I have had my little sister "beat my face," as the kids say (do my makeup up really nice, for those *not* familiar with teenage slang).

Long story short, we ended up messing around in the car, and although these kinds of things with Felix had always been much more tragic than they were hot, this time it was not only hot but HAWT. "What is happening right now?!" I thought.

But that same night, he told me not to post a cute photo of us I had taken at the restaurant, claiming he wanted to keep a low profile, and it all came barreling back at me like tennis balls from a shooter. It also dawned on me then that he really should've offered to come to me or at least meet me halfway rather than having me drive so far on all those crazy highways so late at night on a school night. That would've been the decent thing to do.

So there it was: Felix hadn't changed at all. He was still cheap, immature, and self-serving as he ever was. But dammit all to hell if he hadn't gotten significantly cuter and thicka than a snicka!

Not long after that simultaneously fun and annoying encounter, Felix moved to Miami and almost immediately contacted me to hang out. And for as long as I could muster the strength to do so, I tried to avoid him and make up any excuse not to see him. I didn't want to be mean (feeling the need to constantly please people is a serious problem I have, but am always working on!), but every fiber in my being was screaming at me to stay away.

It's so weird. I'd been very drawn to Felix, and at the same time, I almost hated him. Shit. Not almost. I did hate him. But it was still so, so hard to say no to him. I was good at not initiating contact myself but never great at declining his efforts to connect. Luckily, during that time, I had a few back-to-back trips both for work and for pleasure that gave me time to stall.

But as soon as he knew I'd be back, there he was again. Asking when we could hang out. So we hung out. A lot. We went to the beach and to the movies. We had lunches and dinners. Sometimes we even had breakfast. We went to museums and sat on benches to chat. We had work days at Starbucks (I worked from home, and he was applying to jobs).

Sometimes we'd end up hanging out three times a week—and if we weren't hanging out, we were texting about everything under the sun. He met my family on several occasions and kept close tabs on me during a hurricane scare. He was my date for my sister's wedding. He took me to dinner for my birthday and even had the waiter surprise me by bringing out a dessert with candles. The staff didn't do the happy birthday song thing, so he sang it to me himself.

Then, on the day of my actual birthday, he hung out with me at the beach with my family visiting from Cuba. And even though he only joined us for lunch, because he had to work on job applications, he carried our cooler all the way to the sand on a steamy Miami summer day, in jeans and a T-shirt, before turning around to go to Starbucks, where he waited for us to be ready for lunch.

At first, and for many weeks to come, he would annoy me so badly I often wondered what sort of insane-level masochist I had to be to put myself in this position over and over again. During one of our many outings, I sat with him on the beach and was so out-of-my-mind irritated with him that I legitimately closed my eyes, and in what felt like the wildest inside screaming I had ever done, I prayed to God for *new* love. "Please help me stop going back to these fools. Please help me find new love. Healthy love. Please help me stay away from him. I can't. I can't. I can't stand him! Why am I here?!"

When I opened my eyes, Felix said, "Whoa, you really got lost there." I smiled and lied through my teeth. "Oh I just lose myself when I'm by the ocean," I explained, which is true, but in that instance, I had certainly not been meditating or doing anything else the least bit peaceful. And even though after that very trying afternoon I got somewhat better about trying to politely blow Felix off, a few weeks later, I was saying "yes" again.

But the more we hung out and the more "dates" we went on, the less irritated I was and the more I started to see different sides of him. Sides that were more open, sweeter, kinder, more generous, and full of what almost felt like an effort to be a better version of himself, for me.

I started to feel like I could call him out on small things he did that'd upset or hurt me, and he would try to do better the next time. I felt like I could be more myself, more open, more unglued, and more imperfect. I felt like I could talk to him for hours on end and he would listen. I felt like I could have a drink and he wouldn't judge me. I felt like I could reach out if I was upset about something and he'd be sensitive and caring enough to engage me in comforting conversation.

Inevitably, the more I experienced this different version of Felix, the more, to my horrified surprise, I began to fall in love with him. Suddenly all of the things that used to make me roll my eyes seemed like cute quirks—all the reason to love him more, not be annoyed with him. I couldn't wait to talk to him again or make the next plan or get that next tight, warm hug.

The day everything changed, I woke up thinking to myself, "Fuck, I'm screwed. Completely and utterly screwed." It was a super sunny Saturday afternoon. The kind that fills you with life while simultaneously pouring red hot heat through the fibers of your jeans onto your suffocating skin and back out through your shiny pores. We'd made a date to go to a new science museum downtown, and I didn't think anything of it.

We'd been on these friend dates a dozen times before, and nothing had happened. I'd even started to feel like we might have truly developed some kind of real friendship. And even though there'd been many moments of sexual tension between us, I was glad it hadn't gone past that. It was the healthiest way to keep this thing—whatever it was—from blowing up like a fiery hell. Over time, Felix had become slightly less irritating and had even become a fun buddy to do activities with—he was always down for an adventure, and I really liked that about him. This might be OK after all, I thought. But then we messed up and messed up big.

That afternoon at the museum, something between us started to shift. He was being friendlier than usual; sitting really close to me, taking pictures of me and with me, and sharing food with me. And none of it was bothering me, which came as a complete surprise. In fact, I felt butterflies in my stomach as all the walls I had put up to protect me from this very strange yet adorably goofy man began to crumble like an old, dry cookie.

That day we did the museum; grabbed lunch; caught a movie; and, at the end of the night, sat on a bench talking and simply spending time together. I felt like I might explode from the want to kiss him, but I held strong. "This will not end well," I kept telling myself. "It's not worth it."

But when we got back to the car, he made a move, and it was the hottest kiss Felix and I'd ever shared. Still, after my initial loss of sense, I pulled away. My heart was beating out of my chest, and even though all I wanted to do was cling on to those suddenly sexy lips for as long as possible, my gut was screaming bloody murder for me to stop.

The tension in that car on our drive to drop him off was so thick I could barely breathe. And eventually, as I often do, I gave in and suggested we move this party to a hotel, where I could feel more comfortable than making out in a car like a teenager. We were both living with family at the time, so that was the only option. He shyly accepted, and we pulled over to see what hotel we could find at a reasonable, last-minute price.

We quickly found something affordable, and decided to book it and split it. When we got there, the room wasn't ready because we had just booked it a few minutes earlier, so the hotel staff offered us two drink tickets for the wait. I was incredibly nervous, so I very much welcomed the offer. I ordered the strongest drink I could stomach, an apple martini. I know. I know. I'm so hardcore. But I'm not a huge drinker outside of wine and beer.

So I guzzled that martini down and ordered a second while he sipped on a beer (he barely drinks at all). Soon I was super relaxed and enjoying his company in what felt like very rare form. Although I usually felt a little uptight and self-conscious around Felix, this time I felt so free and close to him. And we had an amazing night together.

What started with the best kiss we'd ever shared ended with the best sex we'd ever had. It was then, in the midst of that surprisingly romantic tangle, that I began to feel something frightening. And in that scruffy hotel bed that night and the next morning, I knew—despite all of my better judgement, the years of trying to avoid him or at least not take him seriously, and feeling fairly certain this could never happen to me no matter how much I messed around with that fire—I had effectively fallen in love with Felix. And while it felt like a nice story of unconventional love and overcome obstacles to tell our grandkids one day, it also felt sickening, strange, and just plain *wild*.

But wait, it gets better (or worse, depending on how you look at it). Over the next few months, things got increasingly strained between Felix and me. For me that night at the hotel had signaled a clear shift in our relationship. But for Felix, it was still clearly a struggle for him to face both his feelings *and* the mess we had admittedly created together.

Our interactions became more and more laced with an insurmountable sexual tension every time we stood close to one another. We began to hang out and talk more, to the point that it felt like we were in an actual relationship. The only problem was, after the night at the hotel, there was never another kiss, touch, or move made on either of our parts.

And, trust me, it wasn't because I didn't want to. My growing feelings and the immense chemistry between us was enough to make me crazy, but I couldn't bring myself to make a move and possibly face rejection. Because, even though I had somehow fallen for Felix, I still hadn't forgotten who he could be, and I wasn't willing or interested in even the slightest possibility of facing the wrath of another one of his cruel emotional outbursts. So instead I died a little each time we said goodbye with only a hug that felt like it could kill me every single time.

I finally found the nerve, under the influence of one large birthday drink (this is the same birthday I mentioned before), to bring up the gigantic elephant patiently sitting at the corner of every room we filled. It was somewhere between the meal and the birthday cake that I asked the infamous question: "What are we doing?"

As pure fear swept across his gaze like fire quickly engulfing a forest, I continued to speak, bringing up our rendezvous two months prior and explaining that I was confused about what we were or weren't doing. It felt like a lot more than a friendship, and while things between us continued to escalate in some ways, in other ways they felt stunted. I also explained that I was baffled at our goodbyes, always filled with an attraction-ravaged awkwardness but never ending in a kiss, much less in anything else. And that's when Felix did the most Felix thing he could do, declaring in a fumble that he wanted to marry a Haitian girl (he's Haitian).

At this point I was fairly tipsy, so instead of immediately seeing right through the gigantic crock of shit that had just escaped his mouth and rushed onto my birthday cake, my eyes watered. What does that even mean, he wants to marry a Haitian girl? That I could never be good enough for him because I'm not Haitian? First of all, in all the years I had known Felix, I'd never once heard him say such a thing, and his brother married a white girl, so I knew it wasn't some kind of family tradition or requirement. Lies. All lies!

Later in that same conversation, he admitted he had no idea why he even said that and that he didn't mean it. He instead wanted a quick way to escape what he apparently deemed to be an unbearable conversation. He apologized and thanked me for having the guts to bring up difficult topics, because he was terrible at it. No shit Sherlock.

So fine. I let it go for the moment. And we agreed to continue to hang out, be friends, and maybe once in a while hook up. That always sounds like a great plan until you actually put it in motion, doesn't it?

But on we went. Still pretending like everything was normal; still hanging out and talking all the time; still sharing looks and accidental touches that left us both smiling and tingling like lovers; and still having awkward goodbyes filled with tension and, sometimes, once he was out of the car and out of sight, even tears. And no matter how much his fear wanted to make me (and himself) believe we were just friends, we were obviously more. It'd become too late to pretend or to run away from what was so clearly in front of us.

After seeing how physically uncomfortable Felix became that first time I tried to have The Talk with him, I was hesitant to try again; really, I was afraid to lose him. Afraid to lose my movie buddy, my adventure companion, my partner in dreaming, and my calm-me-down-when-the-world-got-me-down confidant. I was afraid to lose what had genuinely, much to my surprise, started to feel like a full-fledged boyfriend.

Still, as the days went on and the sinking feeling in my heart started to grow deeper, I knew what I had to do, whether I liked it or not. Because if confronting the situation meant I would lose him, I had nothing but an illusion anyway. Given that our previous conversation on the topic hadn't gone well, I decided to share my feelings in the best and clearest way I know how—in writing.

So I wrote and edited, and I wrote and edited, until it felt nearly perfect and all-inclusive of the torrid situation we had unwittingly created. I explained everything; how, because of our past, I hadn't taken him too seriously over the years and always held him at arm's length. I explained how I was hesitant to give in to his requests to hang out when he first moved to Miami and how little by little, and especially after our hotel rendezvous, I'd started to fall in love with him.

I also explained that I knew Miami wasn't his long-term goal, and I would never want to be someone who kept him from his dreams, but at the same time, didn't we deserve a chance at what could be something really amazing? I told him I couldn't take it anymore and that it had become excruciating for me to pretend everything was normal and easy, because it was anything but.

Then I really put it all on the line: I asked him to be truly and completely honest with me. "Please don't give me any of that 'I want to marry a Haitian girl' bullshit," I asked. And as I waited patiently (or not-so patiently), I braced for the worst while still hoping for the best. I was hoping for the best parts of him to reply to my desperate, hopeful plea for answers and the worst parts of him to stay quietly in the past. But as soon as I read his short, desert-dry, and vague response, I knew it was the worst parts of him that had won the battle yet again.

He said he preferred to remain just friends and that he wouldn't give me any specific reasons for this choice, because anything short of telling me he's gay wouldn't be enough for me and would come off as an insult. Funny how he thought his rude, confusing assumptions would be welcome but his truth wouldn't be enough.

Felix was still, and had always been, a gigantic, emotionally stunted fuckboy with a sweet-boy smile, and I had fallen for it *again*. It was almost reminiscent of that scene in the first *Sex and the City* movie after Mr. Big leaves Carrie at the altar and she finds him on the street, gets out of her limo, and proceeds to beat him over the head with her bouquet, screaming with fiery rage in her eyes, "I knew you would do this! I knew it! I am humiliated!" Except, lucky for me, I never loved Felix *that* much, or even close to it. Thank goodness for that.

Yet somehow, someway, even though I had, in my mind, taken things super slow and given him the time and room to show me that he could be trusted, he had managed to lure me into this whirlwind of feelings, at times kicking and screaming, simply to reject me. I was furious. How could this man, who had chased me for six long years, through different cities and even when he lived in a different country—always reaching out to tell me how amazing I am, asking to hang out, sitting ever-so closely, complimenting my beauty, admiring my strength, and incessantly apologizing for how he had treated me back when we first met—now tell me he wasn't interested? How was this actually possible, and how had I let it happen? *Why* had I let it happen?

Once enough time had passed, my rage toward Felix subsided a bit, only to be replaced with rage toward myself. I played with fire, and I got burned. I'd opened myself up to him despite all my better judgment and all of my past experiences with him that clearly told me he was no good. I'd let the excitement of having an adventure buddy and someone to talk to all the time convince me to collapse the walls I had built up to keep him from hurting me again.

I'd let the attention get to my head. I'd let the idea of this relationship and everything that it could've been in a perfect utopian world get the best of me. I'd laid out the path to failure for myself, and I'd willingly walked it, ignoring every sign pounding beneath my feet. I'd helped create this entire situation that I now had so much disdain for, and I had to accept my role in the whole thing. So, as much as I was angry at Felix for what I felt might very well be the greatest lead-on of all time, it helped the healing a bit to take a step back and realize I had it coming. I knew better, and in the end, there was really nothing to be shocked about.

Even so, I was still profoundly hurt, and my ego was taking a large part of the bruising. I'd often seen Felix as a sure thing; someone I could undoubtedly fall back on if I ever got *that* desperate, but the funny thing is, it didn't feel that way at all when it was happening. Instead it felt like some feel-good love story that took hate and strife and turned it into something beautiful. But now that I've gotten distance from the situation through time, I can see clearly that I was 100 percent settling.

He was there. He was available. He was into me. He was always down to go out and do things. And so I had convinced myself to fall in love with this man and make it work, for the sake of the fantasy. And not the fantasy of Felix, because that was never much of a fantasy, but for the fantasy of a relationship—that one thing I'd gone without for what seemed like forever and then some.

So, if I'm honest with myself, I was using him as much as he was using me, although I'll still never understand why he took it upon himself to force his way into my life over and over again if he wasn't looking for any kind of real end game with me. That's the part I'll always struggle with, but at the same time, I'm glad things between us came to a head when they did.

After his blah-blah-blah response that night, I told Felix I was confused, hurt, and needed some time before I could consider any kind of friendship with him. He said he understood and told me to take my time. His calmness was infuriating, but fine.

For several days after, I was miserable. It was a unique mixture of anger, sadness, and broken ego that I wasn't quite sure what to do with, but I sat with it. And after about a week, I was already feeling much better. The anger had dissipated some as I started to realize the sheer absurdity of the fairytale ending I had concocted in my head with this man who was never, ever meant for me and who I knew could never make me happy in the long-run.

So I reached out and proposed that we sit down to coffee, lay everything out on the table, and be completely honest with each other. And if he helped me understand what his intentions had been or why he felt the way he felt, I could get my head around the idea of remaining friends, even close ones. I reminded him that the majority of our issues throughout the years had stemmed from a lack of communication coated in pretense; by always holding back a little, by never being quite real with each other. He agreed to meet and have that coffee with a side of difficult but necessary conversation, but it never happened.

The day I reached out, he said he was traveling home to Chicago and would contact me when he was back in Miami. I think it was three weeks before I actually heard from him with some story about just being sooo busy. Please. No one is so busy that they couldn't find an hour or two to grab coffee and talk if it was at all important to them—that's one thing I've definitely learned time and time again in life. People make time for what they want to make time for. Everything else is at least some form of an excuse.

In that same message, he said he was off on a trip again and wasn't sure when he'd be back but that he'd be in touch to set up our coffee date, to which I responded, "No worries. Safe travels." What I meant was, "Too little. Too late. No thanks." If only I could've said the exact thing I meant, but alas, that's always easier said than done.

The truth is, Felix didn't want to face me or my barrage of questions. He didn't want to open up and tell me how he really felt about these "reasons" he was so sure I could never understand. He didn't want to face the truth. And that's fine. That's his choice. But I wish he would've at least dug deep for the courage to be upfront with me, even if just on a text or an email—anything. I wish, after everything, he would've thought enough of me to think I deserved that much from him.

Later I found out he had gone to Chicago with an open-ended ticket and never returned. And that's when I felt relieved that things had ended when they did. Because that's when it became crystal clear that while I was envisioning the possibility of a future together, Felix was only passing the time during what he considered to be a pit stop in Miami.

How much more devastated would I have been if we'd still been hanging out and talking nearly every day, only to watch him up and leave out of nowhere? Which I now felt sure he would've done, even if we'd still been interacting on a regular basis.

As I write this, it's been well over a year since everything went down, and what I currently feel is a mixture of light disgust and great relief. At the end of the day, Felix and I had a lot of fun together in 2017, so in that sense, I don't regret it. I've also stopped being mad at myself for opening up to him and letting myself fall in love, because it showed me, yet again, that as soon as I think my heart has turned to burnt charcoal and I have nothing left to give, I can still manage to find the kind of openness and forgiveness that made our brief affair possible, and that gives me hope.

Felix has never been the one for me, and he never will be. Once back in our early days in Chicago he told me that I was *almost* "the one," but not quite. Well. You were never even close, honey, so suck on that! He was merely at the right place at the right time, and I'm thankful he didn't allow me to continue on my path of delusion where I had come so close to settling in such epic proportions.

I'm also proud of myself for not allowing him to continue wandering around my life aimlessly and for keeping any small digital interactions we've had since everything crumbled super short and dry. I finally just stopped answering altogether, because it was pointless. For a long time, he often liked my posts on social media too (although that too has pretty much ceased now), which I always found incredibly annoying, but at least I no longer let the attention confuse me. Instead I roll my eyes and keep it moving.

And whenever I do have a flashback moment when I miss or think of him, I just say, "Fuck him!" in my head, and it helps cut the thought off right away so I can continue to move on and not dwell. I used to have those moments a lot more often, but these days I rarely have them at all.

Because Felix's lack of intention, honesty, and commitment isn't about me but about him, I'm afraid to think of how far the charade and the pain might have gone had we continued to play our childish game. After so many years of mostly unwanted contact that I was too punk and too nice to put an end to, I'm glad he's finally out of my life and that I don't have to feel bad about it. If he were to ever reach out and ask to see me, I'm finally and fully prepared to say, "No thank you."

So thank you Felix because I'm finally free, and I learned quite a few things in the process. Mostly I learned that, even when I try to settle, the universe sees to it that I keep waiting for what I really want and deserve, and I am *very* happy that is not you.

CHAPTER 7
Older Men and Dominican Babies: The NYC Scene

Just when you think you've heard every lie in the book, you meet a more creative man.

I arrived in New York City from Chicago in mid-June 2014, and by July, I was already dating. What can I say? I was excited for the change of scenery and hoping, yet again, that things would be different for me in the love lane. My main pipeline? Good ol' Tinder.

There was the guy who looked nothing like his photos (it was definitely him, though surely not in the same year), but he was nice enough that I didn't want to hurt his feelings. We had our one date, and after that we remained sort-of friends who hung out a few times here and there. Thinking about it now, I'm not sure why I didn't just kick him to the curve as soon as I saw him and realized he hadn't presented himself truthfully. I guess it's because I know what it's like to be insecure, especially when it comes to weight, so I chalked it up to that and not any sort of maliciousness. Still that's annoying. Who knows? I might have been more attracted to him had he been honest and had I not felt completely blindsided when I stepped out of the cab to meet him.

Then there was the dentist who felt the need to let me know during our date that he usually dated smaller girls. We had awkward sex once, and that was that. I think he was annoyed by me, and I was definitely annoyed by his highly undeserved arrogance. Next, playa.

After the dentist was the med student who became super aggressive when I refused to let him sleep on my couch (yeah right!). He was way cuter in his photos than in real life. I mean let's be real. He was downright frightening. But, again, he was nice enough, so I mustered the strength to get through the date without making him feel bad.

My thing is, I'm friendly and chatty, and I can pretty much get through a pleasant meal with almost anyone. So I'd rather do that and let the person down easy afterward than to be like, "Hey, I'm not attracted to you. Bye!" I think that's rude if the other person is otherwise perfectly nice. Maybe I should rethink my strategy, eh?

But after dinner, the med student became not so nice very fast. We had a few drinks at the restaurant, and he kept begging to come over and stay at my place in Hell's Kitchen (where we already were) so he wouldn't have to travel back to Queens that night. But I wasn't born yesterday, and I already knew what would happen if I let him come back home with me. The couch would soon turn into my bedroom and my bed, and I would be in an extremely uncomfortable situation.

So yes, his phone was dead and he wasn't entirely sure how to get home (he hadn't lived in New York for long), so I did feel a little bad for him, but hell no. I felt less sorry for him when he started yelling, "What?! You're not into me?! You don't like me?! Fine! Go!" So I left his drunk, hateful ass on a stoop and power walked my butt the block or two home, hoping to stay out of his sight and out of his life forever. And, luckily, I did. I hope he woke up the next morning safe, at home, and at least a little ashamed of his behavior so that he never scared another woman that way again. Wishful thinking, right?

Then I caught a little break, or so I thought. My next suitor was one of those rare, perfect-on-paper guys who I thought might just change everything once and for all but ultimately just left me disappointed, disgusted, and rolling my eyes so far back in my head that I hurt myself a little every time I think of him.

Jamaican Lies

Marcus was tall and handsome, with caramel skin lit up by the melody of his apple green eyes and a smooth Jamaican accent that could pierce your soul with a simple "Hello." The man was fine, fine, fine. He was smart, too; Ivy League educated and in the process of getting his PhD while teaching undergrad—the man of my dreams. He was sexy, sharp, ambitious, and island-made. Damn.

Marcus and I also met on Tinder. It took us about a month to figure out a good time to get together, but one Friday night, we finally did. I ventured out to meet him near Columbia University. He rolled up in his car and asked me to get in so we could find a restaurant. I had second thoughts about getting in a car with a stranger, but the moment I saw him in person, I felt an overwhelming sense of attraction and calm. So fine, I got in.

A few minutes later we were sitting across from each other giggling and carrying on like a pair of overexcited school girls. We were both so immediately entranced by each other that we could barely manage to have a real conversation in-between all of the blushing and flirting. "Sorry, you're so damn beautiful, I'm having trouble focusing here," I said. He smiled and said he felt the same about me. Eventually we both came down from our highs and were able to chat and get to know each other a little. This man seemed too good to be true, but I let the experience wash over me anyway. It felt too damn good not to.

We continued to see each other for about six months after that night. The hangouts didn't happen as often as I would've liked, but Marcus was a busy man. Between studying for some classes and teaching others, he didn't have much time to get together. And, for the most part, I was OK with that. I was still reeling from a major heartbreak in Chicago (*My Funny Sad Life: I Once Loved a Sociopath*), and I wasn't looking to get serious with anyone too fast. It's really the only reason I survived Marcus's eventual and unique deceit as well as I did; I had kept my heart at arm's length for the first time maybe ever, and it served me well. Progress!

Marcus was perfectly nice to me, and when he couldn't hang out because of work or school, he'd apologize profusely. He'd call me to tell me that he cared about me and he didn't want me to think that because he was busy, he wasn't interested. He told me he was always thinking about me and needed a little patience and time until things could get easier and more frequent between us. He said I meant something to him, and he didn't want to lose me. OK, fine. Again, I wasn't in any rush, and although I liked him a lot, I wasn't sweating him like that. I appreciated what I thought was his honesty and transparency, and I stayed (relatively) calm.

Still part of me felt like there was something Marcus wasn't telling me. I'd go to his apartment and jokingly ask if he was hiding a wife or a couple kids in the closet, and he'd look at me like I was crazy. One time he got really irritated, looked at me like he had never looked at me before with scorn in his eyes, and said, "Stop trying to figure me out. You can't." At the time, I wasn't sure what he meant, but now, duh! He was basically saying there *was* something to be figured out, and he was not a fan of my looking for it.

The other issue between us, or maybe more so for me, was that Marcus didn't like to kiss. He indulged me a few times at the beginning, but it quickly became pretty nonexistent—I'm talking not even a peck. He had a damn good reason for this, but it was still a huge problem and a daunting barrier to any real intimacy between us.

Marcus told me that when he was a little boy back in Jamaica, he had a maid working in his home who would pin him down and kiss him all the time. Horrific, yes, but I had a hard time accepting that he wouldn't at least try to go to therapy and attempt to work something like this out, as I had done for many of my childhood issues.

Today, removed from the situation, I worry that I might've not been sensitive enough to the issue and maybe focused too much on how it affected me, but to me, having sex without kissing just makes it feel dirty. It also makes it hard for me to connect, and it made things awkward—still enjoyable in a purely physical sense—but confusing in an emotional and mental sense.

But despite it all, things felt positive between us. Although maybe that was because I wasn't taking it too seriously. And when the day came that he finally sat me down and let that skeleton I'd been searching for out of his tightly shut closet, I felt more distraught by the fact that yet another romantic entanglement was blowing up in my face in the biggest, most humiliating way *again* than by the fact that I was losing him.

It was January 2015, and we had both just returned to New York after separately visiting family in Florida and Jamaica (or so I thought—he had even sent me pictures!). He came to see me one night, and everything was lovely. We sat on the couch facing each other, sipping wine, chatting, flirting, and smiling from ear to ear at each other as we usually did. But then the bomb hit.

"I have to tell you something," he said, his relaxed expression suddenly turning serious as his eyes filled with worry.

"OK . . ." I said.

"I have a son," he said. "He was born December [insert date here]."

"Wait. What? As in December 2014? Like a few days ago?"

That's when Marcus explained that he had in fact gone to Jamaica, but only for a couple of days at the beginning of his trip. The rest of his holidays were spent in the Dominican Republic for the birth of his child. Come again?

I was in complete and utter shock. "I don't understand," I said. "Where did this woman come from? How did you meet her? Where has she been this whole time?"

He then proceeded to tell me a whole sordid story about how he met her while on vacation in the Dominican Republic and had actually known her for quite some time. Then he said she was already three months pregnant when we met.

I sat there stunned, looking at him like, what in the actual fuck, dude?

The best part is that he insisted I really had nothing to be upset about. It had nothing to do with me, he said. He was not *with* her, and no one knew—not even his mother.

"You're not fucking your mother!" I yelled. His eyes were like an alarm blaring, flashing red. Deafening.

In-between my rage, anger, and confusion, I cried. I couldn't believe I was back in this place again—sitting next to a man who had lied to me in the worst way and made a complete fool out of me in the process. I couldn't believe I had once again fallen for a man who had promised me the stars and the moon (in due time, anyway) but was full of horrible lies and shiny bullshit the whole time. And even though I hadn't allowed myself to fall in love with Marcus, I was distraught. Not so much about him but at the sickening pattern that had taken hold of my love life for so, so, so fucking long. Even when I took things slow and protected my heart, I still wound up broken.

I still slept with Marcus that night in a drunken rage. I guess it was my way of saying goodbye. So when I discovered his broken bracelet in my sheets the next day, I texted and asked him to remind me of his address so I could mail it back to him.

"Mail it?" he asked. "Damn." He knew I was serious about ending things between us. And mail it I did. Along with a little card (I keep stationery on hand, folks!) with something like, "Here's to everything we never were and all that we could've been." I'm so dramatic, I know! But I wanted to make a statement. It made me feel better.

I never entertained any kind of relationship with Marcus after that, but we did sleep together a handful more times in the next few years, because, again, this is what I do. And every time it sounded like a much better idea in my head than it actually was in reality. Quick. Awkward. All about him. No kissing. Totally not worth it.

He never stopped reaching out, sometimes with outlandish requests that only an epic dummy like Marcus would make. One of those times he asked me if he could declare me as his child's babysitter on his taxes. What? No! Another few times he asked me to invest in a new product he had developed. Again, what? No! First of all, I don't have money like that, and second, if I did, why in the hell would I "invest" it in the most untrustworthy man on the planet. Brother, please. Get a grip, playa!

Other times when he reached out he'd ask to see me, telling me he wasn't romantically involved with his child's mother, as if to comfort or entice me. And if I was craving the company or sex enough, I'd give in. I actually think the first time I said yes, come over, after everything went down, was a year and a half later, the night before I left New York to move back to Miami. Damn it. I stayed strong for so long!

And the second I locked the door behind him on his way out, I regretted it. Because of course he would show up super late, even though he knew I had a lot of packing to do and was catching a flight to Florida the next day. I would also have to deal with a moving truck and clean my apartment before heading to the airport—all by myself. It was so inconsiderate, but also my fault for even entertaining this dumb idea of some grand goodbye that was never merited and so irrelevant at that point in time.

I saw Marcus two more times over the next year and a half during work trips to New York. I'd feel lonely and reach out, because I knew he would come. The first time was OK. Quick. Awkward. All about him. The usual. But the second and last time, I opened my door and had to take a deep breath to stop myself from laughing; he had dyed his hair a clownish shade of blonde. And he legitimately looked like a black Bart Simpson. I. Could. Not.

It's almost as if his foolish mind had made its way onto his once magnificent exterior and ruined everything once and for all. There he stood—a puddle of the beautiful man I had been in awe of during our first date that warm summer night a few years before.

And the sex? It was impersonal to the point of discomfort. I'm talking mechanical; devoid of any connection or consideration whatsoever. My body didn't feel like a body, it felt like a pawn. He slammed me into the bed from behind, and I never even saw his face. I tried to relax and enjoy what I could until it was over, but, lord, I had rarely felt so cheap and inhuman.

There was, however, one thing that night I was proud of myself for. You see, beyond the no kissing, Marcus never put any work into the sex at all, but he always expected me to go down on him. Like clockwork, he'd walk in the door, say a thing or two, take off his pants, and assume the position. But this time, for the first time, I said, "No. We're not doing that tonight." He was SHOCKED. "Come on," he said in a whiny whisper. "Nope. You have your rules? Now I have mine." Mic drop, bitch!

Perhaps that's why the sex ended up feeling the way it did. Maybe he *was* mad at me for rejecting his selfishness for the first time and, as a result, was being more aggressive than usual.

In any case, he left me that night never to be heard from again. And I'm so glad it's finally over for good. He must have felt it too. We had officially stretched this shenanigan between us as far as it could possibly go; we'd sucked that peach pit dry and then some. Or maybe it was just my first "no" that did it. That usually does the trick. The second I stop giving in to doing things their way, that's when men (and sometimes women) finally leave me alone.

And I can't for the life of me figure out why it always takes me so damn long to make what seems like such a simple, liberating move. Maybe it's boredom. Or insecurity. Or maybe, just maybe, it's all an intense case of terribly misguided hope. Believe it or not, I do get better at letting go of terrible people (or just terrible *for me*) all the time, in my own baby-step kind of way, so at least I'm grateful for that. Onward and upward, right?

Thank you Marcus for the illusion you fed me—it was really nice while it lasted. And ultimately, it made me stronger. So much so, that now, whenever I think of you, I mostly just laugh. You're *so* cancelled boy—BYE!

Old Dildo

After Marcus there was Martín, a 50-year-old Dominican guy with the maturity of a horny teenage boy—and the sense of one too. But man, did he make me laugh. They always get me with the laughs!

Martín and I met at a club in Midtown Manhattan on bachata night. He came up to me toward the end of the night and asked me to dance. I was skeptical from the start, but damn it all to hell if he didn't look as fine as cherry red wine. His shiny shaved head, crisp white suit, and smooth-talking demeanor reeked of player of the century, but it was also strangely intoxicating.

We spent the next hour or so twirling around that dance floor like two trees swaying in the wind. He asked me my name. I asked him his. He asked me where I lived and where I was from, what I did for work, and how old I was. And he actually seemed disappointed when I said I was 30. He was feeling pretty good about canoodling with what he thought was a girl in her early 20s. Sorry not sorry, dude. (This happens to me all the time. What can I say? I get it from my momma!)

I took Martín home that night, and shit got weird fast. First he took off my boots and commented on the musk—then he laughed about it. What is it with these men?! I'm sorry that I'm a human and I sweat a little in tights and boots, especially after a night of dancing. Damn. Can a girl catch a break? But OK fine. I think I told him he could leave if he had an issue, to which he said he was just making an observation. Observe and be quiet, fool! Please and thank you.

But wait. It got weirder. He insisted we take a shower before having sex (and it had nothing to do with the boots). "Um, I *just* took a shower a few hours ago before the club," I protested. But he insisted, and I thought well, OK. Maybe this will be sexy or whatever.

Cue the most awkward shower of my life.

This man actually proceeded to wash out my lady parts with a loofah almost as though he thought he could turn it into a peach ready for the snackin' by doing so. Talk about a mood killer. Then he proceeded to shave said peach. I stood there, kind of going with the flow while trying to focus on the sexy naked man my eyes saw and not the strange, neurotic one seemingly prepping my body for surgery.

Eventually we actually had sex, and it was good (OK, great), but after everything it took to get started, it hardly seemed worth that whole show. To make matters worse, he kept complimenting his own cleansing work the entire time like, "Damn I did good. It's so fresh." I'm sorry, but if you need to rid lady parts of every semblance of nature, then maybe you don't like them? Maybe you should grab an apple instead and be on your merry way? I'm just saying!

Apparently, even after all that, I was still amused by Martín. I think I was attracted to his quirkiness and the fact that he made me laugh constantly with his antics. We ended up hanging out for about three weeks, during which, in true Sonia style, I started to think I could really fall for him. Could I deal with the fact that he was 20 years my senior and had kids just a few years younger than me? Maybe it would be OK, my ever-idealistic heart thought.

But alas, Martín quickly ended up annoying the shit out of me with his antics, demands, and comments about my weight. One night as he laid next to me mere minutes after devouring my body, he said, "You need to lose weight, baby," as he spooned me. Yes, as he spooned me! Really dude? If that wasn't enough to send me straight into a red-hot rage, he swiftly proceeded to tell me about his adult daughter's similar weight struggles. Can a chunky girl live, though?!

Now, I'm not one for confrontation, but I immediately hopped out of bed, threw on a T-shirt, and asked him to leave. "I can't believe you are kicking me out right now," he scoffed, "This has never happened to me before." Well there's a first time for everything, *baby*.

He had also showed up to my house that night with a half-full bottle of vodka and a gift—a humongous vibrator/massager with extensions that looked more like Smurf kitchenware than something intended for pleasure. And all of this was after knowing him for a grand total of about two weeks. The best part is I still have that thing in a box somewhere, although the thought of going near it fills me with tempered disgust. But I hate to throw away a perfectly good piece of equipment, you know?

Then there was the time he was blasting music in his car so loud and driving scary-fast down already-intimidating Manhattan streets. I asked him to please lower the music a little and slow down. His response? "Listen baby. This is who I am. If you like it, good. If you don't, too bad." OK. No one asked you who you are or are not. I asked you nicely to turn the music down and slow down so that my head and heart could stop pounding out of my body. Thanks!

And THEN there was the time when he again compared me to his adult daughter. I had taken a photo of our appetizer at dinner. It was a pretty plate. Sue me. But don't constantly compare me to your daughter. That's creepy, sir. Very creepy. It's almost as if he saw her when he looked at me, which, wow. No. Just no.

Eventually I also found out that Martín wasn't even this man's real name. It was something completely different. Think Jon versus Leonard. Nothing to do. He also apparently had a couple of girlfriends. Yes, a couple.

So after a wild and interesting-to-say-the-least three weeks, which felt like at least 10, we called it quits and went our merry, separate ways. And sure, I missed the way he made me laugh, his passion, and his wild side, but I *did not* miss the man child in my bed, the doctor in my shower, or the father all up in my insecurities.

Like all the men (and the women) before him, I heard from Martín a few more times in the next few years, who asked to see me and let me know that he thought about me often. And, although I considered meeting up with him during one of my trips to New York, it thankfully never came to pass. In fact he messaged me on Thanksgiving in 2018, and I never responded. What's the point? And why do they hang on for so long after we only dated for a few weeks? Why?!

Sigh. Another day. Another playboy. Thank you Martín. For nothing.

A Nice Surprise with Equal Demise

After Martín (or whatever his damn name is) came a most unexpected surprise—Julian. This surprise came swiftly and left me in much the same way in summer 2015. He was a temp at work who had apparently been around for a while, completely unbeknownst to me. Julian wasn't the kind of guy I would've ever noticed or stopped to look at twice.

Skinny, short-ish, and snow white-ish—not my type at all. But his sweet, shy guy deal and ability to make me laugh in that makes-you-feel-so-alive kind of way lured me in. I think it was the way he looked at me, too, and the way his brain stimulated me more than most men's bodies had before.

I learned of Julian when I was asked to consult him about a project. I set up a time to meet. I'll come to you, I noted in the calendar invite. When the time came, I walked over to his general vicinity, scanning the name plates on the outside of each cubicle.

"Hi, I'm Sonia," I said, popping my head in when I finally found his cube. His big blue eyes smiled and signaled me to come on in. I sat down next to him and, almost immediately, sparks were ricocheting off those three little cube walls—but I wouldn't notice it until after I walked away.

From that first interaction, he made me laugh so hard, at everything, practically the whole time we were together. And it was all so refreshing to feel this sudden attraction to someone so effortlessly and unexpectedly, especially because we hadn't met through an app. For once it felt simple.

Still I didn't think much of our first meeting. I was mostly grateful for the laughs and distraction. At the time I had been going through a rough spot with my roommate, and the levity Julian brought was much needed. It wasn't until he started putting lunch on my calendar and we began going on coffee or walk breaks almost every day that I really started to feel something was a' brewin.'

I looked forward to those breaks so much. We had a unique flirtation and chemistry that could melt away even the most stressful or gloomy day. Plus it was new; exciting; and, best of all, easy. Before I knew it, I had fallen—hard—for this sweet, dorky, wonderful (or so I thought), not-my-type-at-all man.

I knew I was smitten for sure after work one night when we were hanging out in New Jersey. First we stopped at his apartment so he could shower and change. He had planned to ride back to the city with me after dinner to meet up with some friends. At his place, he showed me videos of him rapping. Yes, rapping. He was good, though. I was impressed. It was a little corny, but somehow it made me like him more. I'm a sucker for creative types!

Then I sat in his living room and hung out while I waited for him to get ready. "Damn, he cleans up good!" I thought as he walked out of his bedroom decked out in a long-sleeved plaid shirt and jeans, smelling like fresh, delicious maaaaan. Damn. Damn. Damn.

I told him he looked really good. He smiled and said, "Oh yeah?" But we continued to pretend like there was nothing going on between us, much like we'd been doing up until that point. And out we went. Both smiling from ear to ear. Both pretending.

We had tacos and a couple drinks. I was chatty, as I tend to be. He pissed me off for the first time by asking me why I always felt the need to fill in the silence. "I don't know," I said. "That's what you do when you're out to dinner with someone. You chat. You don't just sit there in silence. That's awkward."

I guess he wanted to take in the moment, which was fine, but if we were still pretending we weren't on a date and just two friends hanging out, then I'm sorry if a quiet, romantic dinner was making me feel a little nuttier than usual.

Eventually we moved on and enjoyed the rest of our meal. Afterward we hopped on the train, and I swear he sat so close to me he was practically on my lap. All right then. He must be trying to tell me something, I thought. We talked and laughed as we always did, but this time with our faces so close I could feel his breath on my lips with every word. I expected him to kiss me any second. I felt it in my bones.

But alas, my bones were hopeful and *wrong*. His stop came, and off he went with nothing but a smile and a wave. All right. Just kidding! Still I felt the butterflies buzzing around in my stomach. Whatever this was, it was getting closer to coming to fruition. It was just a matter of time, I thought, with a confident smirk showing its arrogance on my face.

Unfortunately things did not go the way I planned. Instead Julian became more and more aggressive. Suddenly he was mean. He'd snap at me for little things and get easily offended by almost anything I said. What changed? Why did he suddenly seem so agitated? What had I done or said? I was being the same person I'd always been. I didn't get it—not for the life of me.

So I decided to speak up. But I didn't quite have the balls to do it in person, and I wanted to give him time to react. So I sent him an email one evening with the subject line "Elephant in the Room." I explained that I was under the impression that we were friends, good friends at that, and I was confused by his recent behavior. Maybe it's because there's something more than friends brewing here, I asked?

Then I confessed that I did have feelings for him and I was fairly certain he felt the same about me. I suggested this might be the cause of our growing tension and basically asked him to face the music with me. I concluded the message by saying that I could accept if I'd totally misunderstood things and would be OK remaining friends if that's what he wanted. I was sure that wasn't the case, but I felt like I needed to end my ballsy note with a save of some sort in case a nasty wave of rejection was coming my.

I pressed send with my hopeful heart in my throat, and it wasn't long at all before that same heart fell to the floor and deflated with disappointment—again. I had misunderstood, he said. He felt pressured by me, he added. He hoped we could still be friends, he concluded.

Pressured? Man, I felt bad. But wait. I hadn't been the one initiating consistent lunches and coffee breaks. I'd never been the one coming to look for him or chasing him. I'd never asked him for anything but the truth and the possibility to end our ill-fated dance, which was making me crazy. But maybe I *had* imagined the whole thing. Maybe I was coming off the wrong way. Maybe I was the bad guy here. Ugh!

Needless to say, I pretended to be OK with everything and agreed to remain friends, even though I knew, with 100 percent certainty that would never be the case. Things had gotten too real. He could no longer hide behind his facade. And I did initially try to stay friends, even though things had fundamentally changed and soured, but his aggression toward me continued to escalate and eventually I got fed up. Fed up with his bullshit. Fed up with him.

The end came one day when I confronted Julian about something mean he said to me and explained the way it made me feel. His response was something to the effect of, "You know you make up scenarios in your head and then eventually make yourself believe them, right?"

Excuse me? Rude!

Now, at this point in my life, I had been gas lighted and emotionally abused enough to know that this man was officially a dick. He was being verbally and emotionally abusive, and he had to go. So I let him know that and stepped back. I stepped back completely.

After that when he'd see me in the halls, he'd give me this bone-chilling look that would've made any witness assume I had murdered his mother. It was a look filled with a fiery hate I don't think I had ever seen in anyone's eyes before, not even Tafari's, way back in 2009. And every time it happened, my body felt a little chill run through it, but I'd look away and keep walking. I'd carry on. I'd laugh it off. What choice did I have?

Luckily his contract ended, and I no longer had to see him. Things went back to normal for me around the office, and slowly but surely, as I always do, I healed. And when I thought back on the whole thing, mostly I laughed. What a psycho, I thought. Another bullet dodged. Another story to tell.

But to *nobody's* surprise, Julian made a brief cameo in my life a few years later after I had moved back to Miami. He messaged me one day and apologized for how things had gone down between us. Sound familiar?

He then confessed he had indeed always had a huge crush on me and that he didn't know how to deal with it, especially while we were still working together. (By that time, I already knew; a mutual "friend" told me that he would kick himself and say things like, "She's so pretty. I like her so much. Why can't I just ask her out?") He further confessed that he frequently spent time looking through my Instagram photos, thinking about how sexy I am. Then he told me he was coming to South Florida to visit family. He wanted to see me and try to make things right between us.

So, in the spirit of forgiveness and the repeated dumbassery that I have spent my life committing by letting these fools back in again and again and again, I agreed to meet him for drinks. I was nervous, but five minutes into it, things felt like they always had when they were good. We had drinks and appetizers and then chatted and laughed while sitting by a fountain surrounded by other flirty, giggly fools.

Eventually I asked him to come home with me (I would be there alone that night), to which he nervously agreed. Once we arrived, we sat on the bed for a while chatting more—my mind mostly focused on when he would finally, after all of this mess, kiss me. But he didn't. Instead he suddenly and awkwardly—mid-conversation—jumped off the bed and practically ran down the stairs and out the door, leaving me to feel rejected, dumb, and completely unnerved.

But fine. I went to bed with my boggled mind and called it a night. The next day I messaged Julian and confronted him about the whole thing. "Why would you reach out to me after all of this time, move the conversation 1,000 miles per hour, tell me how much you always liked me, and track me down in Florida just to reject me?" I demanded.

That's when he reverted back to his trusted pattern of evading any and all responsibility for his actions and turning everything around on me. He said I was acting weird the whole night and that turned him off. So once again, he was too much of a punk to face his feelings for me and make his move and instead hurled insults at me, making me feel like a monster. I was upset, but that's when it finally sank in: this guy is insane, and he'll never change—it's time to let it go for good, and so I did.

Julian messaged me a few times after that, but it always ended in a fight, and I told him it was obvious we would never be able to get along so we should probably stop trying. And that's the end of that. Another day. Another maniac. Another story. Another lesson. Another end.

Thank you Julian for reminding me, once again, that hurt people hurt people and that emotionally abusive folks like you should be left behind the first time they attack, not the second, third, or fourth time. I hope your future is led by the best parts of you, and not the worst. Good luck and God bless!

Sweet, Spanish Hope

My next glimmer of false hope came later in 2015 during my stay in Miami for the holidays. I met Yoan through a relative's boyfriend when my New Year's Eve buzz had prompted me to ask to be set up with someone.

By the time Yoan arrived at my parent's house where we were all celebrating, my buzz was wearing off (I had done entirely too many tequila shots and Modelo Especial chasers). I was ready for bed! But my relative's boyfriend insisted we all go hang out at her apartment with them. I had sobered up by then, and my dad still wasn't comfortable having me drive myself, so I ended up going in the car with Yoan instead. Essentially I was now trapped.

We got to the apartment, where we all hung out and listened to music for a while. Eventually everyone else went to bed, leaving Yoan and me in the living room to our own devices. He was cute, but man, I was tired, and this was hella awkward. He had also come from Cuba not long before and didn't speak English, and although I'm fully bilingual, I struggle when I have to speak 100 percent Spanish in a social situation—especially a brand new one like this. I'm used to only doing that with my parents and other family members. It's the Cuban American struggle.

So we continued to talk for a while, and suddenly he asked me if I thought he was cute. I said yes, and in he went for the kill, also known as the first kiss. Cool, cool, cool. This was getting increasingly hotter, but I still wasn't sure I wanted to sleep with him on someone else's couch. Then he whipped out his penis and ever-so confidently and nonchalantly said, "This is what I got."

Being the size queen that I am, I immediately said, "Leggo!" Well played, my friend. Well played. He obviously knew exactly what he was doing, although I imagine that could've gone a very different way for him with someone of different preferences or tolerances.

Surprisingly everything was quite nice. He made love to me like he had known me forever. He was sweet, gentle, and all-around delicious. Woooo. Just the thought of it brings back good, tingly memories.

Yoan and I would spend the next two days holed up in the same living room together. The whole group barbecued and hung out by the pool. We drank and carried on. And when the others went to bed, we'd stay up and talk for hours. He told me about his whole three-month ordeal leaving Cuba and making his way to Miami, with a stint in St. Thomas in-between, where no one spoke Spanish, yet he still managed to work and find a place to stay. I was inspired by him. And I was grateful that he wanted to share all of these intimate, difficult stories with me. There was definitely a connection beyond the hot sex and large member. And, once again, I thought that despite our differences and the odds, this could turn into something.

Unfortunately a few days later, I had to head back to New York. But for the next few weeks we'd talk on the phone every single night. He'd usually call right at 6:00 p.m., when he got out of work, but at that time I'd typically still be at work or be waiting for my train on a noisy subway platform, so we'd have a quick hello and check-in, and I'd call him back when I got home.

It was amazing. We talked about anything and everything. His life, my life. Our aspirations. He'd give me advice on some of the harrowing harassment issues I was having with a neighbor and some other folks. He even gave me advice about men in general. He was worried about me, and it felt so genuine; not like someone who was trying to tell me what to do, but like someone who was looking out for me. We also talked about when I might come down to Miami again to see him and how he'd always dreamed of visiting New York. I told him I could teach him English and help him figure out culinary school (he was a chef in Cuba but working in landscaping in the United States).

I had known Yoan for all of two minutes, but my ever-hopeful, lovesick heart was ready to put everything into making it work, because I had so much trust and faith in the connection that we shared and the effort I saw him put into maintaining it, even from a distance. To be honest, I also think I was clawing for any reason to leave New York, where I had grown fairly miserable, and move back to Miami. Maybe people wouldn't judge me for giving up on the big shiny apple if I did it for love?

Unfortunately (or maybe fortunately, in the end) after about three weeks of being back in New York and sharing our long, soul-feeding, daily telephone calls, he was suddenly nowhere to be found. I didn't get my usual 6:00 p.m. check-in call. I started to worry, but I gave it time. Then, around 9:00, I messaged him and asked if he was OK. Nothing.

A day or two later, I messaged him again. I was worried, I told him again, although I was starting to wonder if he was fine and his disappearance was something else. He could've easily said he was no longer interested instead of disappearing, I told him. I thought we had something—at the very least a nice friendship, I added. I don't deserve this, I concluded. But no response. Ever.

I was heartbroken, probably more so because I was going through such a hard time in life overall and having someone like him to talk to and feel taken care of by felt extra good and necessary to me. Then there was the all-too-familiar, I can't believe this is happening to me *again* breakdown that comes each time a new love bubble of possibility pops loudly in my face, almost as if to say, "Gotcha!" with pride.

The best part was Yoan was still hanging around my family, and no one said a word. It was too awkward, I guess. And when I saw him a good year and a half later at the wedding of the same people we had met through, he tried to act like he didn't know me. But I looked good as hell that night with Felix accompanying me as my date, and I wasn't going to let Yoan get away with it. I was going to make him face me.

So I went up to him and said hello. He acted as if nothing had happened between us and nervously tried to retain his composure. He had gotten married some time before (not long after we met), and she was there with him (maybe that was the cause of his sudden disappearance?). He gave me a kiss on the cheek and asked how I was. I responded politely and smiled, and the interaction was over before I knew it. But he spent the rest of the night staring at me as I danced with Felix. He also tried, to no avail, to be super cool every time I caught him doing so. And that was enough vindication for me.

That night I felt like Yoan knew exactly what he'd lost, and I was happy. I moved back to Miami a few months earlier. I'm not sure why I ever thought I needed a reason like him to come back and rescue me from New York. Oh Sonia, Sonia, Sonia. I could and would rescue myself like I always had. Sometimes I forget how strong I am. I guess we all do.

Funny enough, Yoan works in my neighborhood, and I've ran into him a few times while walking my dog. The last time I saw him, he awkwardly came over, gave me a kiss on the cheek, and asked me how I was doing. He sweetly pet my dog, and we exchanged pleasantries for a minute. Then, as I walked away, he yelled, "¡Te quiero!" or "I love you!" (Although "quiero" has a lighter meaning than "love" in Spanish, if that makes sense.) I just kept walking. These men, I tell ya.

Thank you Yoan for giving me a sweet fantasy to lose myself in, albeit momentarily, when I needed it most. I know now that you are yet another dodged bullet, but what we shared was still sweet, and I remember it with delight. Thank you for not choosing me. I am at peace knowing that you realize what you lost, and I wish you the best. I hope you make all of your dreams come true, and that you are happy and well. Buh-bye!

Thin Romance

After Yoan ghosted me and I remained in New York for another nine months or so, I encountered my last attempt at dating there—Roberto. We actually met at the same club I had met Martín. What can I say? Bachata night was my jam. Roberto wasn't my type either; kind of lanky and delicate, but his eyes twinkled (I'm a sucker for that twinkle!) and his lips were filled with sweet, delicious promise. He could dance too—a sure path to my heart!

The first thing that struck me about Roberto was his hard-to-believe sweetness and romanticism. This guy cannot be for real, I remember thinking as he swayed with me on the dance floor, held my hand, kissed me as though he had loved me for years, and even drew me a napkin masterpiece to take home. I think it had the day's date on it along with our names and some of the first words we had shared. I mean! Who does that?

But I tried to relax and let the rarity of the moment wash over me with enough idealism and hope to make me momentarily forget everything I had been through.

That night, after a few hours of dancing on this cloud of delusion, Roberto walked me to my train and kissed me goodnight over and over again. He didn't want to let go, and I didn't want to stop believing he was real.

Later that week, we went on an amazing date; a real date. He even planned it, something I've often found myself doing for other men. We had dinner at a quaint but fancy candlelit Italian restaurant in the East Village, where we talked and drank for hours until the restaurant started to shut down around us. It might've been one of the best dates I've ever been on.

Then, just as we were deep in dinner and conversation, he asked if I'd ever been married or was married. Confused, I said, "No, and why would I be here with you if I was married?" Then he sort of smirked and said, "I'm married." My heart sank. I had been down this road before, and I didn't want to be on it ever again. When he saw my face contorting in confusion and quiet rage, he said, "I'm just kidding!" Um, not funny, sir. Not fucking funny!

I continued to feel a little uneasy after that, but he reassured me it had been nothing more than a bad joke, and eventually the date got back on track. After the restaurant, we headed to a similarly quaint cocktail bar, where we cuddled and kissed in a corner booth while sipping our sweet, colorful drinks. Soon, after a little convincing on his part, we were back at his place. It was a one bedroom he shared with his brother, so his bedroom was the living room. But his brother was with his girlfriend and wouldn't be home that night, so we had free reign of the place. Or so his story went.

We listened to music and he showed me his paintings. Yes, Roberto was an artist. He did graphic design to pay the bills, but on the side, he was an incredible creative. It was all so romantic and beautiful. I completely fell for every single bit of it, and soon I also fell into his bed, or in this case, his close-to-deflated air mattress (basically the floor). We made love that night, and although his rail-thin body made my riper figure feel somewhat like an elephant on a tightrope, it was still quite lovely.

I didn't sleep well. I was on the floor, after all, and my back was killing me. But it was nice to wake up next to him and see the sunlight bounce off the faces in his paintings from a distance. We laid around for a while, kissing and carrying on, and when my back couldn't take it anymore, I said I had to go. We got dressed, and he walked me to my train, holding my hand and randomly stopping in the street to passionately kiss me. "Is this guy for real?" I asked myself again.

Well ladies and gentlemen, as it turns out, he wasn't. I never saw Roberto again after he dropped me off at the train station that afternoon and said, "I can't wait to see you again." We texted a bit, and he kept saying he was busy with this or that through incredibly long texts that would make you think he actually had real intentions of seeing me again. Part of me started to think maybe he wasn't kidding when he joked about being married, but I would never know.

Either way, as it turns out, Roberto was a farce like all the ones who came before him—just a more romantic one. Once again I found myself significantly affected by something that had lasted about as long as a manicure.

Because, as usual, it wasn't about the man himself but the deeply painful, discouraging pattern: yet another failed illusion, another rejection, another couple of weeks wondering what I did or said or am that brought me to this fate one more excruciating, life-questioning time.

Per usual, there was no one around to give me any answers, only time to help me move on from beating myself up for this constant ill fate when it came to my never-ending search for love—a fate that couldn't seem to move past a beginning into a middle, but always straight to the end.

Luckily, or maybe not so much so, I spent my last six months in New York too consumed by survival to date and too traumatized by incessant street harassment and impending bankruptcy to worry about dating. But that's a story for another time and another book!

Thank you Roberto for showing me some new moves. Next time I see them, I'll know to ask more questions!

CHAPTER 8
Miami Dater's Nightmare, Part 2:
Come-Out-the-Woodwork Creeps

Creeps keep just as well in the sunlight as they do in the cold.

Since I've moved back to Miami, dating has mostly been a series of ill-fated attempts at recycling past loves (e.g., Nathan, Felix, and Julian—with Felix definitely taking up the most time, energy, and heartbreak of the three). Then there's been the dating apps, ghosters, and all-around weirdos.

One guy, a violinist, I spoke to every day for about four weeks. We even spoke when we traveled, and we shared photos and videos often. When our schedules finally aligned, we made a plan to meet up for dinner and drinks. Like clockwork, he started being weird and distant the night before. But all right. I tried to stay calm. Then, being the planner that I am (in addition to the girl who's been burned one too many times by inconsistent men), the next morning I messaged him and asked if we were still on for our date that evening. Nothing.

Once again, for the umpteenth time, I was crushed by another disappointment. Funny enough, though, a month later I was in Mexico for a girlfriend's bachelorette party when I received a long, tedious text from him. He apologized profusely and told me he had disappeared because he was too afraid of rejection. Really people? We're all scared. That doesn't give you the right to treat someone like trash, but all right. That's cute. Then he asked for a second chance.

I replied because I was intrigued by this madness. I told him I had no hard feelings, because, at the end of the day, he was no one and we were nothing. I asked him why I should even consider giving him a second chance. If he had royally disappointed me the way he did before I even got to meet him in person, what was left for me to believe in or expect from him? Nothing.

He kept texting me, and I started to waver, but I eventually told him I wasn't interested and it wasn't going to happen. I surely wasn't going to sit there and do to him what he had done to me by leading him on. The whole thing had simply lost its luster, and no amount of apologies or explanations could make me want to try to meet this person again. At least I was finally (finally!) starting to do better. Look at me go!

Then there was the sexy real estate guy, who ended up being another fuckboy royale. We met on an app and got lunch soon after. Immediately we hit it off. He was handsome, educated, and had his shit together. That same night, he messaged me to tell me he really enjoyed my company and wanted to see me again. I liked his style. He wasn't wasting my time, and he was direct; he was letting me know how he felt and what he wanted. Finally, right? I told him I liked him too and would love to see him again soon.

We lived far from each other, and we were both busy with work and travel, so coordinating schedules was no small feat. Eventually I agreed to make both of our lives easier by coming to his apartment for movies and wine for our second date. I was bunking with family at the time post–New York, so it made more sense for me to go to him because he lived alone.

As soon as I walked into his apartment, I was impressed. I had never seen a man's apartment look this put together. I'm talking matching furniture. Fully equipped kitchen. Clean everything; the smell of scented candles caressing the air throughout the entire space. Damn. He became 50 times hotter than he already was.

He was sweet too. We sat on the couch with our wine and picked a movie on Netflix. We cuddled on the couch. We talked about life. He asked me if I wanted children. I said I love children but wasn't sure if I wanted my own anymore. He said he wasn't sure either.

Eventually we made our way upstairs, where he pulled out all the stops. Everything was perfect. The candles. The silky-smooth sheets. The goodie drawer open and ready for business at a moment's notice. His kisses. His touch. His unique, whoa-what's-happening-right-now-but-wait-I-like-it approach to foreplay. Pretty soon I was melting like butter on a piece of toast.

After the deed was done, we stayed up cuddling and chatting. We even talked about wanting to be open and direct with one another. I asked about his thoughts on us sleeping together so fast. "Be honest," I said. I was worried; as a woman, if you really like the guy and sleep with him quickly, you're always at least a little worried, even when you know you shouldn't be. (Again, blame it on the patriarchy!) He said the last time he slept with someone right away, he ended up dating her for five years, so that never made a difference in his mind. OK, cool. I cautiously believed him. It was comforting.

The next morning, we hugged and he said, "I'll see you soon" as I made my way out the door. But I never saw the man again. There were maybe two more texts before he ghosted me. Not again, I thought. Like seriously. What in the actual fuck? Sigh.

Months later, I saw him on a different dating app, with his age listed as a few years older than on the app we met on. On *this* app, he also listed himself as a father. Like come on, dude? Do you not realize that the same people are on different apps, just like you are?

I knew it wouldn't change anything, but I wanted him to know he was caught red-handed. So I messaged and said, "Wow, so that's why you disappeared. Because you're a liar. Glad I don't have to feel bad anymore or wonder what I did wrong." I felt truly disgusted *and* vindicated all at the same time. At least the sex was good! I gotta count my wins, right?

Somewhat simultaneously there was another guy I talked to constantly for several months, including sending pictures and videos (PG stuff!), who I never met because he kept putting it off. We ended up getting in an argument after a while, not because he had avoided getting together but because he was being an arrogant asshole, and even though it felt silly to once again talk to someone for a long time without meeting, I was glad I had the chance to figure him out before I wasted any real-life time. He also definitely reminded me of Tye in more ways than I was comfortable with. Next!

Then there was a guy who lived in Chicago but was allegedly trying to move to Miami. We met on an app one weekend when he was in town but didn't start talking until he was back in Chicago. Within a day or two, he called me and we spoke on the phone for a while, which is uncommon for folks you meet online these days. To be honest, I don't love talking on the phone, and it feels especially awkward doing so with a stranger. But I appreciated his desire to connect in some kind of real way, and so quickly too.

He was a teacher and coach by day and a financial trader by night, and he had a young daughter. He also had a fairly problematic situation with his daughter's mom, who he said was on a lot of drugs. But all right. He laid it all out on the table and was trying to be upfront. At a certain age, if you're still single, it's kind of expected that the people you date will come with some baggage. Lord knows I'm luggin' around a couple large and bursting-at-the-seams suitcases myself.

When he came to Miami again to apartment shop, we made a plan to meet. We actually ended up going out on his birthday, which was kind of a strange circumstance to meet somebody for the first time, but we had a great time. We drank, danced, talked, and even got caught in the rain. We kissed in it too. It was as romantic and deliciously cheesy as it looks in the movies! I think that was a first for me.

We were under a small awning hiding from the rain when we had a run-in with an obviously drugged man, who said something crazy to me. My date got physically in-between the guy and me, and the man immediately shut up and walked away. I'd be lying if I said it wasn't super-hot—to have my date jump in to defend me like that. Although I was also thankful that the guy just walked away. I would've been mortified if things had escalated. I'm a lover not a fighter, people!

Later that night we hung out a little bit with his cousin, and with nowhere to be alone, we (thankfully—who needs *another* notch on this bedpost, right?) only ended up doing a whole lot of kissing in the quiet common areas of the apartment complex. And at the end of the night, we said goodbye and promised to see each other again soon. But surprise, surprise: we never did.

We continued to chat for the next few months until his next alleged visit, during which I would've already moved back into my own apartment. We had planned to have him stay with me, which was a little much for someone I didn't know well, but I was trying to be open to the possibilities and not give into fear. Plus we had already met in person and hit it off.

But the week of that alleged trip, he started to act strange and pull away. I had also started to feel like some of the things he'd say and do were suspect. So when he didn't message me until the day he was supposed to arrive to tell me he was "really sick" and wasn't coming, I was annoyed but almost relieved. I had also last-minute adopted a precious Chihuahua that same weekend (hey Ms. Ginger!), so I had bigger and better things to do anyway!

Even though I was almost expecting a cancellation and didn't care much at that point, I was still left with the same usual questions—what happened? Did I do or say something to turn him off? Was he hiding something the whole time? Is he crazy, or am I? Who knows, but another one had bitten the dust, and I had become a pinch more cynical in the process. These boys really ain't shit, I thought. Oh well. Puppy!!

After that dude, I had two or three other dates and quickly fading, empty, or all-around unsatisfying rendezvous and a couple more dating app ghosts, including a guy who texted me for almost a year but never came through on meeting up. I guess I kept entertaining it because I thought, "What the hell else am I doing?" But after enough disappearing acts, I finally accepted the ridiculous futility of it all. Then there's the beautiful Eastern European doctor who I stopped talking to when he insisted that if I get complimented or catcalled 100 times in a day, I should say "thank you" 100 times a day. Nope. Not even close, motherfucker. Not even close.

One of the latest, and all-time faves, was the other "doctor" on Bumble who responded to my message of, "Try not to judge me too much for starting a convo this way lol, but damn you are sexy. And apparently smart too. Are you a unicorn? [smiling face with sunglasses emoji]" with, "Lol, no, but I know you got a nice ass. Send me a pic of it [heart eyes emoji, kissy face emoji]. A pic of that ass bent over." Really dude?! How did he travel from my cheesy intro alllll the damn way to that? I can't even, folks. I really can't even.

And last, I *have* to mention the guy who legitimately threatened me with Trump during a date. This guy (another app guy!) was being super loud and obnoxious at the bar where we were having our first date. Initially I was trying my best to go with the flow and chalk his behavior up to nerves. But when he started embarrassing me, low-key whispering threats about a random lesbian couple nearby who wasn't bothering him in the least bit or even looking in his direction, and essentially making fun of me for being short, two seconds after telling me how beautiful I am, I had to say something.

So when I told him he was doing entirely too fucking much, he said, "Well I'm white, and you're not, and Trump is president, so when shit really starts to go down, I'm gonna be good and you'll be screwed."

I cannot make this shit up, my friends! I was *shocked.* Here I thought I had heard and seen it all, but Trump's America said, "Hold my beer," and showed me! I laugh about it now, but wow, that night I was completely beside myself at his reaction and his words, because, again, what?! Best part is he tried to reach out again a few weeks later. Boy bye!

CHAPTER 9
34 Times Exhausted

Never been a quitter, but I still know when to quit.

And that, ladies and gentlemen, brings us to the present day—a strange place of dating peace in which, yes, things are molasses slow as far as my love life goes, and sometimes I feel the boredom of a pretty nonexistent love life poking at me like a skewer stabbing a shish kebab steak, but the drama is on a strict diet, and I'm *not* mad at it! In fact, I finally feel free. And on most days, as long as everyone I love is healthy and happy, my next trip is booked, and my bank account looks good, I feel pretty damn great.

That's because I'm no longer sitting by the phone waiting for anyone. I'm not crying over love songs—but instead enjoying them again. I'm not pining over this guy or that guy, or longing to be attached. I'm not going on bad date after bad date, or desperately shuffling through dating apps to find "the one." And I don't need a man to make me feel beautiful or worthy or loved like I once did. Best of all, I'm not putting up with anyone's shit. Thank you sweet baby Jesus! It's all part of a relief I long yearned for, but never imagined I'd actually get. And it feels damn good.

I'm generally not even interested in sex either, mostly because whatever sad, tired mess is attached to that penis, is entirely not worth it. These guys can't even seem to properly carry out a booty call anymore, even when they're the ones initiating it—they say they're coming over, and then they never show up. I mean, seriously? Ain't nobody got time for that, honey.

I think things really started to slow down for me after Felix. Once I began to wake up from that pathetic illusion, I struggled to wrap my head around how I had arrived at a place where I almost settled for someone I have always, deep down inside, practically hated since the first time he showed me who he was years ago. I didn't even know I was desperate enough to put a nice little bow around a love story (any love story, obviously) that I was actually willing to convince myself that Felix might be *the one* after all. Good God almighty!

That's the thing. For yeeears, I chased tirelessly after this idea of love that I was so convinced could somehow complete me or save me. Always single, but perpetually wrapped up in these crazy unhealthy, super long-winded and utterly unfulfilling situationships with mostly terrible people. Looking for worth in others' eyes and arms. Measuring myself against the attention I received from men. And worrying I must be a broken person because love never worked out for me the way it always seemed to do for others.

For so long, I was constantly haunted by the ghost of all these miserably failed attempts at love. And the pain followed me everywhere. Everything was a trigger—a persistent reminder that something must be deeply wrong with me. It's actually kind of fascinating *and* horrifying when I think about it. But you know what? I'm over it. All of it. Thank God!

So I don't try anymore, and people usually have lots to say about this hands-off approach. They tell me not to be so negative. They ask me if I've tried this or that to meet someone. "Have you *really* tried though? Have you *really* put yourself out there?" they ask. Then they search for a way to make it my fault that I'm single, but they assure me I won't end up alone. "Not you! No way. Never! You're too amazing," they insist.

But here's the other thing: I'm not being negative. I'm being realistic. And I'm giving myself a flippin' break (I mean did you or did you not just read this book and all of my wild stories?). There are far worse fates than living out the rest of my days as a single person. I've spent two decades being positive about love and trying to see the best in others. I've also spent the better part of those two decades giving said others chance after chance after chance—being open to forgiveness and to the fact that people are capable of change, only to then be told I'm "too nice" or "too open," and once again, it's all my fault.

Further, I've spent those two decades trying not to be "too picky." Trying to look past crystal clear inadequacies and afraid to ask for too much or to think of myself as superior in any way. Afraid to think of myself as deserving of someone who is perfect *for me*. Because when I do those things, people tell me I'm single because I'm not willing to compromise. But then if I settle, even just a little bit, they say, "That's your problem." You're not selective enough, they'll demand. I mean seriously. A girl can't fucking win!

And, yes, I actually have tried everything, thank you for asking. I've met men through school, work, family, and friends. I've dated men of practically all ages, backgrounds, education levels, professions, and ethnicities. I've gone to singles and speed-dating events in three different big cities. I've been on and off every dating app known to humankind throughout the course of a decade or so, and even met people through AOL chat rooms when I was waaay too young to be messing with that stuff in the first place—scary! I've even fallen in love with a couple of my gay friends before—sometimes before I knew they were, other times, not so much! I was *always* searching.

I've slept with some people right away, and I've waited a few months (or years) to sleep with others. I've stayed open to people whose qualities lie outside my "list" of qualifications, and I've also stuck to my list religiously in other cases. I've been completely honest about who and how I am with people, and other times I've held off a bit to ease 'em into it. I've followed my heart by jumping on trains, buses, and planes to believe in love at every chance, and other times I've been extremely cautious with each small step (e.g., Marcus and Felix!).

I've taken deliberate breaks from dating and sex to heal, find myself, and recollect myself. I've spent time in therapy working through my issues and being honest about the part I play in all of this, and all of the mistakes I've made along the way. I've learned to do better, and I've worked endlessly through the years to build my confidence and fully learn to love myself. Yet I still get the tired, "You'll find love when you *truly* learn to love yourself." Seriously, fuck off. I'm human, and will *always* deal with a certain degree of insecurity, doubt, and vulnerability, but that doesn't mean I don't love myself. Hell I'd marry myself if I could! Trust and believe.

But none of these strategies has worked as far as finding and having a successful relationship goes. I've also been through a lot of creepy situations with men, where I have felt uncomfortable, violated, and even feared for my physical safety and at times, my life—excuse me if I have some trust issues! (Actually they're not even "issues." They're fears based on actual patterns of experience!) So yes, I get irritated when people point a finger and blame me for remaining single or ask me a million and one questions about what I have or haven't done to make it work.

I'm not perfect, just like any other living being, and I've certainly done my fair share of fucking up. Who hasn't? I have *many* flaws, and I try to be self-aware about them so I can catch myself when I make a mistake and work to do better next time. I also make a point to apologize when I need to and recognize how I could've gone about doing or saying something in a better, more productive way. I try not to hurt others (getting better at this with age!), and I try to take responsibility for it when I do. And when I can't do so directly, I take it up with God.

So yes, I shut myself down and give up on love at times. Yet I still believe in love. I really do. But there are also many days when I feel like it might not be in the cards for me, and I have to be OK with that. I'm not going to lie down and die because romantic love hasn't worked out for me and never might; I'm going to live and try to be happy with all that I do have, because I am beyond blessed. It took me a long time to see that.

Also I'm fucking exhausted, folks. Exhausted! I don't know if my heart can survive one more beat down; one more, "You're so amazing, but…" I don't know if my sanity can survive one more bad date; one more ghosting situation; one more lie, or one more dummy saying or doing something mind-bogglingly outrageous, disrespectful, or just plain gross. I. Cannot. Take. It. Anymore. Why is that so hard to understand or accept?

Why can't I be tired? Why can't I be angry and disillusioned? Why can't I be over it? Why can't I focus on other things and goals? Why can't I live my life contently alone? At the same time, why can't I be salty at times that every Tom, Dick, and psycho from my past seems to find love, and I can't even get a second date despite being what I think is a pretty decent, if not awesome, human? Why can't I be strong and independent and still crave love sometimes?

Why is all of this (very human) complexity so blasphemous to others? So hard to understand? Because it doesn't fit the box of what society thinks life is all about? Because it doesn't conform to the traditional view of relationships? Because sometimes the truth is much uglier than the fantasy we convince ourselves of? Because

I'll be more honest and vocal about it all than most people? Maybe.

I don't have (even close to) all of the answers, but I know this: I am 34 times exhausted (one for each year of my life), and I don't think anyone should look down on me for that. I've been out here on these mean streets hustling for love my whole life, and I damn well deserve to walk away from it all if that's what my body and my soul are craving. Let a woman live—please and thank you! And if someone were to come along who could make it all seem worthwhile, I'm game. But until then, I'm not playing games with these "children" anymore. I just don't have it in me now, and I am so unbelievably grateful for that—why waste my time?

CHAPTER 10
13 Key Lessons I Learned from 20 Hectic Years of Dating

On the other side of pain, there's clarity.

1. Finding love is a total crapshoot.

I used to think that my treacherous history with love and the pattern of incessant failure that has plagued me, no matter how hard I tried to be and do better, meant I was cursed. I also thought it meant that something was wrong with me. Often I even convinced myself that things might be different if I were skinny. As if only skinny or otherwise "ideally" attractive people find love and get married! (Don't get me wrong. I'm still super cute!)

I guess I felt like if I could figure out why things never worked out for me in love, I could do something to fix it; if I could just figure out exactly what's wrong with me, I could change, and magically fix everything. I'm a problem solver by nature, a planner, and a go-getter at heart. When I want something or I'm not happy in a situation, I devise a plan to reach my goal or leave the situation.

But here's the thing that I've learned after years of looking for something or someone (particularly me) to blame. Finding love is a total crapshoot. It's not always about what you or another person does but about being in the right place at the right time. Now don't get me wrong—finding love and falling in love is all about luck and chemistry, but keeping and maintaining it for the long haul? That's hard work and hard choices.

So if you're still single and surrounded by everyone who isn't, please cut yourself some slack. They're as imperfect as you are and no more or less deserving. It's all dumb luck.

2. There is more to life than romantic love.

When it's real and healthy, romantic love is a beautiful, beautiful thing, and I'd be open to being blessed with it some day in the future, but it's certainly not everything. There's far more in life we can derive joy from, including the various other kinds of powerful love and human connections available to us.

There is a great, big, infinite world out there full of possibilities and adventure that being single opens you up to. If my life doesn't end up looking like most people's in terms of love, marriage, children, and all that comes with those things, I don't have to be miserable. I can still live a fulfilling life packed with purpose. I can have fun. I can connect with others. I can enjoy new experiences. I can laugh and feel grateful. I can be happy. Because guess what, folks? Married people have problems too, and relationships and marriage are not a fix-all for life's hardships.

Regardless of your relationship status, life is beautiful as fuck *and* hard as fuck—for everyone, in different ways and to varying degrees, of course. Everyone, and I mean *everyone*, has problems, and romantic relationships are not served with a side of hot guarantees.

So just live your life, and don't anchor all of your happiness or well-being on whether or not you're in a romantic relationship—there are plenty of people out there who have someone and still aren't happy. Get up every day and do the very best you can with what you have—I promise you there's someone out there yearning for your blessings.

3. The more you have your shit together, the harder it is to date or find love.

As I've mentioned before, for so many years, I spent—no, wasted—all of my time trying to pinpoint the deep, ugly flaw in myself that must be causing all of my misfortune with love. Essentially I was trying to find a reason to hate myself. And for so long, I didn't even think that rather than not being good enough for all of these men, maybe, just maybe, they weren't good enough for me. Because that's not, especially as women, how society teaches us to approach the subject.

Instead we're programmed to doubt ourselves more fiercely than we do anyone else. We're taught to find blame and search for ugliness within ourselves. We're sold promises of confidence and told we're deserving, but we're also shown what happens and the names we'll get called if we get even a little *too* confident.

And the whole time that we're searching solely within ourselves for the obvious clues to our failures, we're often being punished for actually being a good catch; for being too independent, too strong, too vocal, too smart, too everything.

To me the absence of *needing* someone and instead wanting and choosing them is much more powerful. Unfortunately a lot of folks can't deal with that, especially when it comes to a romantic dynamic between a man and a woman. For example, check out these actual things that friends, family, and strangers have said to me over the years:

- "You're too 'woman, hear me roar,' and men don't like that."
- "You need to start putting up with more if you don't want to end up alone."
- "No man wants a woman who doesn't *need* him."
- "You know what your problem is? It's your way or the highway." (AKA, I won't allow the other person to have it *their* way or the highway.)
- "You live alone without a man?!"

Because God forbid that I stand firmly on my own in life and still attract a man into it. But here's the thing that I've learned over the years—finding a relationship that suits you is easy when you're looking for someone to carry you, fill a void, or in some way complete you.

But finding a man (or a woman) becomes far more difficult when you're looking for someone to complement your already great life. When you'd certainly like someone to share the everyday with, but you don't *need* anyone to survive or be happy.

So if you have your shit together and are tired of watching every fool in the world find the love you're searching for, remember that the higher that apple sits in the tree, the harder it is to reach it and take a bite out of. It's those apples hanging loose and low, and fully within reach, that have a far easier time finding hands that will catch them. Oh, and remember, it's also a total crapshoot!

4. People lie and exaggerate feelings and intentions to get what they want in the moment.

People will do and say just about anything they think it takes in the moment to get what they want from you, especially when it comes to sex (men . . . cough, cough) or when it comes to feeding their egos.

When I was younger and didn't know any better, I'd easily get swept up in the idea of love, which was often being sold to me in exchange for sex. I'd make excuses for others all day long and listen to flowery words and promises far more than I paid attention to actions. But words are easy to say. They are, however, far more difficult to back up.

So stay awake folks, and watch for action more than you listen for words. Sometimes the lying or exaggeration of feelings or intentions isn't even conscious, but that doesn't make it any less problematic. Hell I've done it myself at times when I've tried to convince myself that I'm really into someone, because it all sounds so nice and comforting, but at the end of the day, it's the adoration I'm feeding off of more than any actual feelings or plans I might have to see the relationship through.

Then there are the other times when people know exactly what they're doing and don't care who they hurt in the process, as long as they get what they want—whether that be sex, attention, favors, or otherwise.

It's human to get caught up in our egos and ideas of things rather than the reality of them, and I'm learning to pay more attention to myself and others when it comes to romantic interactions. I urge you to do the same.

5. Exes are exes for a reason.

Listen. A man (or woman) will come back into your life as many times as you let him. People like this give you a little time to get over whatever it is they did to piss you off or hurt you in the first place, and then, soon enough, there they are, sniffing around like a dog searching for his bone, and trying to find any opening to make their move. They say they're sorry, they never meant to hurt you, and they've been kicking themselves for losing you. (Oh, how many times I've heard it all!)

"I miss you."

"I've been thinking about you."

"Remember [insert good times or great sex here]."

They'll say they've changed, they've grown, and they have no idea why they treated you the way they did.

And yes, I do believe that people can change and grow (I certainly have over the years), but exes, especially horrible ones, are exes for a reason. In my experience, they come back the same tired version of themselves disguised in shiny new camouflage that'll only crumble in due time. Sometimes it's not even a matter of them being horrible but simply incompatible with your wants and needs. If it wasn't right the first time, it likely won't be the second or third.

Of course it isn't unheard of that two exes reconnect and have a successful, joyous reunion, but I would say that's the exception to the rule. So when that smooth-talkin' ex comes sniffing around, keep your eyes open and your heart on high alert. There's nothing worse than getting your heart broken by the same person twice—trust me. The sheer amount of pure stupid you will feel is enough to make you crazy. And I don't want that for you.

6. Healthy love isn't plagued with drama from the beginning.

Love is hard, but it shouldn't be impossible, especially at the beginning, when everything is supposed to be the easiest. I used to think the more the drama, the more intense or worth it the love was. I guess it probably has something to do with the relationships I observed growing up.

But after 20 years of dating and learning, now I know that a relationship or situationship that starts with a lot of drama will usually stay that way. And it isn't healthy. We all know that love is work, but it shouldn't feel like a constant burden on your life or a daily struggle. And hey, if I'm wrong, then I'll gladly stay single forever. Who's with me?

These days I truly believe that if and when I find the right person—one who will genuinely love me and make me happy and vice versa, it won't be so damn hard. Not all the time, at least. Not right from the start. And certainly not constantly. When it's right, it'll definitely be work, but it won't be impossibly hard work, and it'll feel worth it; it will make me *and* them happy.

Things will just flow, and they won't feel forced. I won't have to beg for affection or commitment, or question every word and every move. And it won't make me miserable every day, either. It's hard to believe I ever thought love was supposed to be that way, but I'm just glad I learned, and can do better now. I hope you'll learn from my mistakes.

7. Real, lasting love exists, but it's not as plentiful or guaranteed as people think.

This realization brings me a lot of comfort, and I hope it'll do the same for some of you. Over the years, I've witnessed a handful of real, loving, and healthy (not perfect) relationships in which two partners have overcome obstacles of distance and fear to grow in love and build a happy life together. So not only do I believe in love but I've also actually seen it take shape before my eyes. It's the kind of love I aspire to but know I might not ever touch.

Many people have this idea that everyone has a soulmate. That it's just a matter of time before any of us find *the one*, and that those of us who end up alone only do so because we're closed off to love or we ruin our chances in some way. But I don't believe that. Love and life are far more complicated than that, and the soulmate idea is a recipe for disappointment that I once held onto for far too long.

Although there might very well be someone out there for me and for others, I don't believe that's true for everyone. And the more we realize that, the less those of us who do end up single will feel the need to berate ourselves or spend our entire lives frantically searching for that person. Instead maybe we can focus our energy on being happy with ourselves and our lives and stop waiting for someone else to make us feel like our lives are worth living. You matter baby, no matter what!

8. When you're too good for someone, they'll work hard to make you feel like you're not good enough for them.

There have been so many times in my life when I convinced myself that a relationship didn't work out or that a situationship didn't evolve into something bigger because I wasn't good enough for the other person. Their behavior and words often made me feel like I wasn't measuring up. They'd make hurtful comments and cut me down in small and big ways every chance they could. I would question myself, and they'd claw at my confidence constantly.

And almost every time, when everything was said and done, I realized that I had actually been too good for them. They wanted to use my vulnerability against me to convince me of the opposite so that I'd stick around for the abuse and never figure them out.

So if you sense that someone you're romantically involved with is constantly trying to cut you down or make you question your worth, realize that it is their own lacking and that they're hoping you won't notice. And get out while you can.

9. A lot of people settle. But you don't have to.

The whole idea that there's someone out there for everyone that I discussed in lesson #7 is further perpetuated by the fact that a lot of people settle. Maybe they don't like to be alone or they start to feel the pressure of being single at a certain age. Maybe they believe that life can't be complete without a relationship, kids, or whatever else comes along with what is considered a traditional lifestyle.

And that's all well and good—everyone is entitled to their choices and to live their lives the way they want. But for those of us who refuse to settle and want to give ourselves the best chance at real, healthy, truly happy, and long-lasting love, it's OK to hold out. So if you're still single, stop feeling like you're cursed, unworthy, or unlovable and start realizing that you're likely just holding out for something better.

I know it's hard. A lot of times I myself question whether I've actually raised my standards, or I'm just dead inside. But I truly think it's the former. I used to practically throw myself at any man who paid attention to me, instead of taking the time to decide if I was really into him too, or just liked the attention. So now, when I don't give into every guy who throws me a glance, it's because I no longer need that validation, and it's perfectly normal not to like someone. Duh Sonia!

Also, as I previously mentioned, relationships are hard as fuck even with the right people. Just think about how complex family and friend relationships can be as we get older and how much effort they require to function and stay healthy. Can you imagine how frustrating and unsatisfying a romantic relationship would be if you settle for someone you're not even fully into or who you're totally incompatible with? No thank you!

10. Desperation is an exhausting waste of precious life.

I spent so much of my young adulthood desperate, and I mean *desperate*, to find love. So much so that I forgot to live in the moment. I can't even count the nights I spent crying, pining, or suffering over one person or another who wasn't worth one tear, much less a river of them. All of it was purely and painfully exhausting. It's like I was torturing myself for something I now realize I have no control over. I can more or less choose how I spend my time, how hard I work to achieve my goals, and how I live my day-to-day life, but outside of that, there's little else I, or anyone else, can control at all, and finding love is at the top of that list.

Finding love is not an item on a to-do list that I can take steps A, B, and C toward completing. It's not a project, a job, or a choice. Instead finding love is up to luck and the universe, and I finally realize all of the desperation I spent so much time on into my late 20s and early 30s was a waste of precious life.

So now I just live that precious life, try not to confuse other people's desperation for mine, and hope for the best every day. Because giving in to desperation is pointless, so instead I'll be grateful for all of my other blessings and smile knowing I'm living my best life.

11. Being alone is far better than being with the wrong person.

Much like any other state of being, being alone comes with its own unique set of challenges. But after feeling more miserable and lonely next to the wrong person on several occasions throughout these 20 tragic years of dating, I now know, with absolute certainty, that I'd much rather be alone and relaxed than dealing with someone's bullshit, waiting nervously for a phone to ring, or planning my entire existence around someone else's feelings—especially when that person couldn't give a shit about mine.

All of our relationships, especially romantic ones, should add to our lives, not take away from them. If a person is only going to bring me problems and drama, I'm better off without them. Plus with all of the married or otherwise spoken for folks who have and continue to come for me all the time (please leave me alone—I am reformed and your advances are depressing as hell!), I'm sorry if I don't exactly hear birds singing when I think of marriage. To be honest with you, there are times, when the whole setup sounds pretty terrible to me. And I get irritated when people speak of this wedding and this prince charming that *every* little girl dreams of. Because as love sick as I have been, *this* little girl never dreamed of those things. Instead she dreamed of feeling joy (something that can be hard to grasp when you struggle with anxiety and depression, and experience a tough childhood) and escaping poverty (#priorities).

Finally, being single is not the death sentence people make it out to be. It can actually be pretty sweet most of the time—you just have to open your eyes to a different way of seeing things.

So until the right person comes along (if they do), you can find me on the couch with my beautiful, loving dog, reveling in the peace of my sweet, sweet solitude, and all the great things to come.

12. Not knowing how to be alone is more frightening than actually being alone.

People often I assume I must be dying inside because I'm 34 and still single, but the truth is it's those same people who cannot, for the life of them, fathom how I could possibly be alone and content who scare me more than being alone ever could.

Because whether you're in a relationship or not, there are no guarantees in life. Zero. Couples break up or get divorced, people die, friends move away, and ultimately the only person you'll have from the moment you're born until the moment you die is yourself. And if you don't know how to sit with who you are, you're in big trouble, honey.

I consider the fact that I lead an independent life a great strength. Over the years, I've learned how to make myself happy and how to make my own plans. And, of course, I love being around people and doing things with friends, but I also love and am perfectly comfortable doing things on my own. Whether that means going to the movies, running errands, or traveling, there is little I can't do and enjoy by myself, and a lot that I actually *prefer* to do by myself. Sometimes I get a little nervous about doing something new solo, but that never stops me. In fact it fuels me.

So if you struggle with being and doing things alone, I urge you to practice. Take yourself out, get out of your comfort zone, learn how to entertain yourself and enjoy your own company, and sit with your thoughts and your feelings. Trust me. It's a skill and a strength you'll inevitably be grateful for. It also makes you feel somewhat indestructible, which is pretty fucking nice.

13. It's a total myth that cheating or otherwise messing up means you're forever cursed in love.

I believe in karma to a certain extent, but this whole idea that if you cheat once or otherwise fuck up in relationships you're cursed forever because of karma is bullshit. I know plenty of people who've cheated or made other mistakes in their relationships (and sometimes are just generally awful), and they still found happiness and redemption.

And here's another bomb for you: at one point or another, most people cheat, whether physically, emotionally, or otherwise—they just don't cheat on everyone they're with. The truth is we're not equally committed to everyone we date, and infidelity is much more common than people like to admit. Sorry. It's the truth. And it's really easy to say you would never do something until you're actually faced with a situation. Trust me.

So if you've done some things in relationships or situationships that you're not proud of, like I have, don't give in to the urge and the societal pressure to punish yourself forever or convince yourself that you're no longer worthy of love or commitment (especially if you're a woman and society is quick to yell "whore!" at every misstep). We all fuck up. It's about how you learn from those fuckups and work to do better that matters. But please don't take any of this as a free pass to be an asshole, because that's not cute either!

CHAPTER 11
Living Single

Sometimes we spend our whole lives looking for something that was with us all along.

Listen. Believe it or not, I'm still very much open to love. I know I've said it a few times already, but I don't think you believe me, so I'm saying it again!

But yes, I believe in love. I'm touched by it. And I celebrate it when it merits celebrating. What I won't do any longer is chase it. I will not define my life nor my worth around it, either. And I will certainly not lie down and die if it never happens for me. Instead I'll be grateful for everything I do have in my life. I'll focus on the other kinds of love that fill my days. I'll focus on offering my best to the world, helping others, chasing my dreams, and taking in the wonder of it all while I can.

To tell you the truth, I've been through so much with love and dating, and I've been single for such a big part of my adult life, that at this point, the thought that I might actually find love—real love—feels out of reach and also pretty terrifying. And not because I don't want it or believe that I don't deserve it, but because I don't even know what that would look like for me after spending so many years watching love unfold "normally" for others while I sat out on the sidelines, almost as if I were watching a movie whose reality I couldn't touch through the screen, no matter how much I reached for it. While I used to carry a deep, deafening shame around my perpetual singleness, now I wear it proudly as a badge.

It's become such a big part of who I am that it's hard to imagine living any other way.

And as far as children go, I honestly don't even know if I want them anymore—although back when I was sure I did, I always wanted two little boys! Go figure, right? Anyway, I haven't had an actual official boyfriend (or girlfriend) in over a decade, and I've only ever been with two people I considered procreating with (although I would never do such a thing with them after knowing what I know now). So tell me: how the hell am I supposed wrap my mind around a baby? I need to wrap my mind around a boyfriend first and work my way up from there. You know what I mean?

People, mostly older family members, ask me all the time what I'm waiting for when it comes to finding a husband. "You're getting older and you'll want to have kids while you can," they say. What if I don't want kids? What if I'm not worried about that? What if I couldn't have them even if I wanted to? Why is it seen as a given that I, as a woman, would be in a rush to have kids in the first place? Why is it so hard to believe that having kids is one of the last things on my mind at any given moment? Instead I spend my time thinking about finances, friendships, family, my health, my dog, my goals, travel, and how I can live a meaningful and joyous life while keeping my mental health as sharp as possible. (So far, I think I'm doing all right!)

The funny part is, people say all of these things as if I could just step out of my front door with a grocery tote in hand and pick up a husband or baby daddy at the corner store. In any case, what they're really asking me is when I'm going to give up the fight and just settle for someone "good enough." The answer is *never*. And if they or anyone else doesn't like that answer, too fucking bad.

I've made it this long on my own, so why would I settle now? I'm used to doing things alone, and I can handle just about anything on my own. I'm by no means swimming in money, but I do OK. I can pay my bills and have some fun, too. And of course it would be great to have a partner to help me with life (mostly someone to pay half this rent and take on some of these dogs walks!), but do I *need* one? No. That and the mere thought of spending time with someone I'm not fully into or who irritates me to no end is enough to send a little throw up into my throat. Been there. Done that. Bought *too* many damn souvenirs.

And having kids can be a beautiful thing (I actually love kids!), but it can also be life-sucking—nobody likes to talk about that. Also I feel like I've spent all of my life taking care of others (i.e., family, and quite frankly, I'm exhausted). So the idea of having more responsibility is not exactly enticing. It's a hard world out there too, one I have trouble coming to terms with myself many days. How do I bring another life into that? I'm honestly not sure.

So yes. I'm human, and I'd like nothing more than to have my story suddenly wrapped up with a pretty little bow, to finally break the pattern of failure in my love life, and to find my happily ever after. But I have to be OK with the alternative and be willing to fight for a full, happy life that just looks different than what many folks expect.

I'll no longer entertain fuckboys or waste my precious, limited time on this earth obsessing about finding "the one." I won't accept disrespect as payment for affection and attention. I won't look away when someone talks to me sideways or treats me in a way that makes me uncomfortable. I won't stay in a relationship that I do all of the work for and have to beg for the slightest bit of reciprocation or respect in. I won't allow deadbeats to take advantage of the little I have, which I've worked tirelessly for my entire life. I won't feel less than because I'm single, and I won't give in to the pressure to settle, no matter how intense it gets at times. Because I am resilient; a light all on my own, and these days there is very little pain left; only hope.

And guess what? As it turns out, none of it was ever really about Luca, Tafari, Isabella or Felix. This entire time, what I was really fighting for at every juncture, after every disappointment, was the courage to love myself—deeply, fully, and without conditions. I was fighting to believe I am enough, and that my happiness doesn't depend on others.

The individuals of my past tried me over and over again (someone hold my hoop earrings!), and each time they tested my resolve to love myself a little more. Each failed attempt at lasting love only pushed me closer to a deeper love with myself, everything that I am, and all that I am becoming. WOW. What a powerful awakening. (Cue that #sosonia salsa twirl!)

Today, I think the only thing that really scares me about staying single is that everyone around me will eventually pair off, build their lives, and have no room or time for little, single ol' me, but hey, I'll make it work like I always have. There's so much to do and see out there in this great big world, that I know I'll be OK. And if that's my cross to bear, I'll bear it proudly knowing that I never gave up on real love, even if it meant going without any love at all. Also, guess what? I'm not a bitter, sad, haggard, man-hating woman. I'm actually a pretty positive, funny, joyful, full-of-life piece of magnificent work on most days, and a damn great catch, if I do say so myself.

So if I do die alone, you can bury me with a salsa mixtape and my self-respect. Aye!

THE END

Made in the USA
Columbia, SC
12 April 2019